Celtic History

An Enthralling Overview of the Celts

© Copyright 2023 - All rights reserved.

The content contained within this book may not be reproduced, duplicated, or transmitted without direct written permission from the author or the publisher.

Under no circumstances will any blame or legal responsibility be held against the publisher, or author, for any damages, reparation, or monetary loss due to the information contained within this book, either directly or indirectly.

Legal Notice:

This book is copyright protected. It is only for personal use. You cannot amend, distribute, sell, use, quote, or paraphrase any part, or the content within this book, without the consent of the author or publisher.

Disclaimer Notice:

Please note the information contained within this document is for educational and entertainment purposes only. All effort has been executed to present accurate, up-to-date, reliable, and complete information. No warranties of any kind are declared or implied. Readers acknowledge that the author is not engaging in the rendering of legal, financial, medical, or professional advice. The content within this book has been derived from various sources. Please consult a licensed professional before attempting any techniques outlined in this book.

By reading this document, the reader agrees that under no circumstances is the author responsible for any losses, direct or indirect, that are incurred as a result of the use of the information contained within this document, including, but not limited to, errors, omissions, or inaccuracies.

Free limited time bonus

Stop for a moment. We have a free bonus set up for you. The problem is this: we forget 90% of everything that we read after 7 days. Crazy fact, right? Here's the solution: we've created a printable, 1-page pdf summary for this book that you're reading now. All you have to do to get your free pdf summary is to go to the following website:

https://livetolearn.lpages.co/enthrallinghistory/

Once you do, it will be intuitive. Enjoy, and thank you!

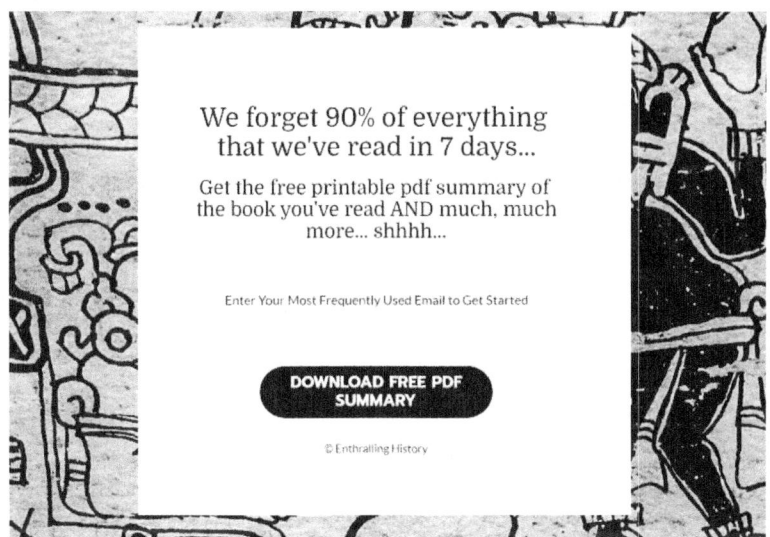

Table of Contents

INTRODUCTION 1
PART ONE: CELTIC IRELAND—THE BASICS (500 BCE–400 CE) 3
    CHAPTER 1: WHO WERE THE CELTS? AN OVERVIEW 4
    CHAPTER 2: CELTIC ARRIVAL IN IRELAND...14
    CHAPTER 3: DAILY LIFE IN CELTIC IRELAND 21
PART TWO: MYTH, FOLKLORE, AND RELIGION 30
    CHAPTER 4: PAGAN GODS AND GODDESSES 31
    CHAPTER 5: TRADITIONAL CELTIC FESTIVALS 44
    CHAPTER 6: CELTIC MYTHOLOGICAL BEASTS AND ENTITIES 52
    CHAPTER 7: CELTIC LEGENDS AND STORIES 65
    CHAPTER 8: FAMOUS STORIES: THE CHILDREN OF LIR, CÚ CHULAINN, AND TÍR NA NÓG 69
    CHAPTER 9: ORIGINS OF THE IRISH LANGUAGE 82
    CHAPTER 10: CELTIC ART 86
    CHAPTER 11: CELTIC RITUALS 92
PART THREE: PATTERNS OF CHANGE (430– 600 CE)....................................97
    CHAPTER 12: HERE COMES ST. PATRICK, 432 CE....................................98
    CHAPTER 13: PAGANISM VERSUS CHRISTIANITY 103
    CHAPTER 14: THE DECLINE OF THE CELTS AND PAGANISM..........107
    CHAPTER 15: CELTIC AND PAGAN INFLUENCE IN MODERN IRELAND 113
CONCLUSION 117

HERE'S ANOTHER BOOK BY ENTHRALLING HISTORY THAT YOU MIGHT LIKE	120
FREE LIMITED TIME BONUS	121
WORKS CITED	122

Introduction

You would be hard-pressed to find anyone in the English-speaking world who hasn't been enchanted by or at least interested in Irish history at one point or another. Ireland is a land of magic, mystery, and ancient customs that reach back millennia.

What makes the Emerald Isle so fascinating can be largely attributed to the Celts, the ancient people who inhabited what is now known as Ireland all the way back in 500 BCE; they even began trickling onto the island as early as five hundred years prior to that.

In the following chapters, we will break down what made the Celts so quintessential to Ireland's history: their daily lives, folklore and Celtic legends, the Celtic language, holidays, and rituals, and what Celtic culture looked like once Christianity arrived on the scene. Fortunately, many remnants of Celtic culture and beliefs remain today, which we will also discuss.

The purpose of this book is to provide an accessible and interesting overview of the Celts, their culture, society, and the effects of their presence, which are still felt today. It is meant to be a historical overview of who the Celts were, how and why they found themselves in Ireland (or Hibernia, as the Romans dubbed it), and what that meant for the people who were already living on the Emerald Isle.

Through this book, you will learn about the Celts in a way that uses easy-to-understand language; you can enjoy this book whether you're a history buff, just getting into learning about your Irish roots, or a beginner at reading about history.

But why should we want to know about the Celts? Any resource about history, especially about a people so influential and pivotal to the course of regional and world events, is essential to understand events that happen around us today. We can only understand the present by first looking into the past. The Celts are the reason we celebrate Halloween each year. They are also the reason Irish Gaelic persists as a language. The Celts left behind intricate metalworking and carving designs, and they may even be the reason Europeans began wearing pants!

This book, *Celtic History: An Enthralling Overview of the Celts*, is the essential resource you need to help you dive into your study of this intriguing and influential culture. Enjoy!

PART ONE:
Celtic Ireland—The Basics (500 BCE–400 CE)

Chapter 1: Who Were the Celts? An Overview

The Celts were really a conglomeration of several ethnic groups and tribes that are now identified as a group of people who shared a common language and linguistic roots. For example, the Gauls, an ethnic group that eventually melded into the Germanic tribes, was a Celtic group conquered by the Romans. Germanic, Roman, and Gallic influences eventually evolved into the French people.

It is now widely accepted that the Celts, although still diverse and widespread in Britain, Ireland, and western Europe during their heyday, were bound together by their beliefs and linguistic similarities.

Who is a "Celt?"

The first time the word we can identify as "Celt" was used to identify a group of people was by the Greek geographer and historian Hecataeus. He used the term *Keltoi* to refer to a group of people who were living in what is now southern France. Herodotus, the famed historian, also wrote about the *Keltoi* in the 5th century BCE.

These people, the *Keltoi*, called themselves Celts. There are several theories on where the name came from, but scholars generally agree that "Celt" is from the Celtic language, not anything that outside people named them. For example, the Apache in the United States refer to themselves as "Diné," which means "the people." The term Apache was assigned to them by their enemies, and fittingly, that is what "Apache" means.

The Celts may or may not have come up with this demonym (a name for a people), but it is certain they used the name to refer to themselves even if they did not originally come up with the name. It is true that the Gauls and Celts were interchangeable in terms of tribal customs, language, cultural similarities, fighting styles, and areas they inhabited. Those very closely related societies only split off after the Roman occupation of Britain and western Europe.

From Where Did the Term "Celt" Originate?

There are several theories as to how the Celts could have adapted the Greek *Keltoi*. One theory is that the name "Celt" could have come from "the offspring of the hidden one" because the Gauls (interchangeable with the Celts when the Greeks wrote in 500 BCE) professed to be descendants of the ruler of the underworld. After all, *Hel* is Germanic in origin and is used to describe the place of the underworld and to refer to the goddess Hela.

Another theory for the name Celt is that it comes from a root word in the Celtic language meaning "to hide" or "to heat." We may never truly know the exact origin of the name, but we can assume that besides it being the Greek term for these western Europeans, the Greek *Keltoi* means "the tall ones."

Whether they came up with their demonym or not, the Celts definitely used that name to refer to themselves. In fact, in what is now Spain and Portugal, the Roman naturalist Pliny the Elder noticed that families used *Celtici* as a surname. This would offer the conclusion that these people identified as Celts culturally and ethnically even earlier than the 1st century BCE when Julius Caesar and Pliny the Elder recorded these findings.

"Celt" and "Celtic" Today

Today, the term Celt refers to the ancient tribes we've been discussing above. The adjective Celtic typically refers to their cultural similarities and art styles, but it more often means a shared language that linked these disparate and far-flung tribes together.

In today's modern world, Celtic simply refers to the languages, cultures, ancient pagan beliefs, inscriptions, and especially the art styles of Ireland, Wales, Scotland, Cornwall, Brittany, and the Isle of Man. These different locations reflect the far-reaching dominance of Celtic culture for what has now been millennia.

Celts and Their Origins

The people eventually consisting of the many tribes and groups eventually known as Celts originated in central Europe in the 13th century BCE, long before they came across the waters to Ireland. The archaeological evidence is scarce and does not start to appear until about the 8th century BCE near Salzburg, Austria.

Hallstatt culture.
Dbachmann, CC BY-SA 3.0 <http://creativecommons.org/licenses/by-sa/3.0/>, via Wikimedia Commons; https://commons.wikimedia.org/wiki/File:Hallstatt_LaTene.png

However, prior to that very well-preserved evidence, we know the Celts migrated from central Europe because we see evidence of their settlements as far as what is now known as Czechia (the Czech Republic). They made their way into western France, and over time, the massive range of Celtic tribes spread all across western Europe. They covered what is now known as France, Germany, Spain, and Portugal.

The Celts made their home in the Upper Danube region. Water is essential to life, and these people found they could trade and travel using the Danube River. They could also use it to irrigate their crops. The early success of the Celts and their subsequent explosion across the

European continent can be attributed in large part to the security and prosperity they received from the Danube River.

It is in this Danube cradle that historians and archaeologists refer to the early Celts as the Late Bronze Age Urnfield culture. The Urnfield name comes from their unique but unified burial practice of burying urns containing the cremated remains of their dead. This way of interring the deceased is pretty much the only extant archaeological evidence of these early Celtic tribes (and remember, the name "Celt" was not used by those people or anyone else for another eight hundred years).

From the Urnfield culture, these people migrated and changed and were then known as the next Celtic bead in the string of Celtic cultures, the Hallstatt culture. This culture was named for the amazing site found near Salzburg, Austria, that we mentioned earlier. This other precursor to the Celts was successful and powerful around what is now western Austria, some parts of Czechia and eastern Austria, Switzerland, southern Germany, and eastern France, which is quite the territory. Those living on the western side of this extensive area were the people who would eventually spread farther west all the way to Britain and Ireland—the official Celts.

The Hallstatt proto-Celts did not prosper from conquest or violence. They did have brave warriors and did not shy away from fights when the situation called for violence, but these people became prosperous because of the incredible mineral ore deposits in the areas they inhabited. These deposits included copper, iron, and salt, which have always been valuable and attractive commodities. The Hallstatts traded with the neighboring tribes and, in turn, received things like gold and amber. In fact, the interspersal of all these goods throughout Europe and even as far south as the Mediterranean (where cultures like the Etruscans lived) helped the Hallstatts have a stable and prosperous existence for close to eight hundred years.

*Hallstatt amber necklace found in a woman's grave.
Wolfgang Sauber, CC BY-SA 4.0 <https://creativecommons.org/licenses/by-sa/4.0>, via Wikimedia Commons; https://commons.wikimedia.org/wiki/File:NBAM_Hallstattzeit_-_Bernsteinkollier_2.jpg*

This trading is evident in gold and amber found in Hallstatt burial sites, as well as Danube iron and copper found dispersed south and east of the Hallstatt territories. The Hallstatts did not die out. As people groups do, they simply evolved and adapted to the times. The Hallstatt culture declined around 400 BCE simply because natural resources started drying up. It was time for a child of the Hallstatts and a grandchild of the Urnfield culture to emerge: the Celts.

Celtic Society

Celtic society operated much like the cultures before it. This was a time before monarchies, dynasties, and feudalism pervaded Europe. This was a time of tribal alliances, relative ease of migration, and flexibility of borders, a time before the Romans became obsessed with conquest and control.

Tribes made alliances through marriages between important members (chieftains' children and the offspring of advisors, the equivalents of nobles and royalty), and these often led to building up trade between tribes. It also meant that if there were intertribal rivalries that needed to be settled through battle, those allied tribes could fight together against a common enemy.

The Celts were many various tribes that spread across Britain and Ireland and western Europe for about eight hundred to nine hundred years, from 500 BCE until the arrival of Christianity in Ireland (but even then, this only shifted their cultural dominance, not the existence of the Celts themselves).

These tribes were never centralized with an overarching ruler or oligarchy, but they were tied together by similar tribal codes, a colorful mythology and belief system, close ties to seasonal changes and the harvest, and, most of all, a common language.

The Celts were organized within each tribe by a hierarchy based on the chieftain's ability to protect the tribe and make wise decisions based on property disputes, harvest activities, and even criminal offenses when necessary. Later on, once the Celts had more interactions (usually in the form of wars or conquests) with the Romans, oligarchical governmental structures began to take shape, although these always retained a uniquely Celtic flavor. The bravest and strongest warriors became advisors to the chieftain, along with the mysterious Druids who led the Celtic religion.

Fascinatingly, the Celts (unlike many of their synchronous counterparts) did not define much of their lives by gender roles. Women and men could inherit property equally, and marriage was seen as a partnership rather than a business or political contract. Women could not be married against their will; a prospective husband needed to have his prospective wife's abject approval before any marriage agreement could take place.

Other than the contrast of women having more rights than their counterparts in other societies, we know little else about how the Celts conducted their affairs as men and women before their arrival on the Emerald Isle. The records are scant, and what does exist discusses a matriarchal society, but these are not from reliable sources, as they come from Romantic authors and early feminists in the last three hundred years.

However, what is mentioned by contemporaneous sources about the Celts is interesting. Strabo, a Greek geographer born in 64 BCE, wrote, "Men and women dance together, holding each other's hands," which was completely unlike the Greeks and Romans. In those cultures, genders were strongly separated by legal and cultural measures. Roman and Greek writers also write of Celtic women being as fierce, tall, and strong as the men, and this can be attested to by the story of Celtic Queen Boudicca, who famously led a rebellion against the Romans in 60 CE.

Although the pagan goddesses the Celts worshiped, as well as the women in their day-to-day lives, had it better than their female counterparts in other societies, this was still a far cry from modern-day women's rights. Whatever was "egalitarian" or "matriarchal" to the extremely patriarchal Greeks and Romans, the Celts' number one enemies, could have been something as simple as a woman not having an arranged marriage. We cannot take these outsider sources at face value—they must always be examined using the lenses through which they were originally observed.

Ancient Celtic Women: Still Largely a Mystery

Because most of what we know about the early Celtic cultures (and we know next to nothing about the Urnfield culture or the Hallstatts) was written by outsiders, we have to take that into consideration when discussing the roles of men and women in society.

The ideal Celtic goddess was powerful, both in war and by her ability to bring forth life—we cannot say for certain that ordinary Celtic women were revered in the same way. However, as we discussed above, Celtic women enjoyed an extraordinary amount of freedom compared to Roman women and especially the Briton women who came after them. "Extraordinary" is a term we can apply liberally. Celtic society was not strictly separated between the sexes like other cultures of the same time, as well as ancient societies that came before and after.

Whatever sources we have that were written about Celtic women were written with the undeniable bias that the Celts, Gauls, and Germanic people were barbarians, and the writers' viewpoints cannot help but be flavored by their own opinions.

For example, Celtic women's ferocity to defend their families and property most likely arose from myths that were extremely popular about the Celts during the medieval period, which came much later than these first writings. The best sources we have to indicate the position of women in Celtic society prior to their arrival on Irish soil are the artifacts that have been found in their gravesites.

As often happened in the past (think the 18th, 19th, and even 20th centuries), archaeologists, all male, assumed that if a grave was decked out with items of precious value, such as weapons, jewelry, and fragments of expensive fabrics, and if the grave was grand and/or intricately decorated, that grave belonged to a man. It is only within the past century or so that anthropologists and archaeologists have bothered to examine whether human remains were men or women.

Since the traditional gender of these buried people has been uncovered, it has been extremely enlightening to discover that Celtic women, especially in the prosperous Hallstatt culture, were buried with full honors and goods for use in the afterlife, such as the enormous bronze mixing krater (a bowl with a handle on either side imported from Greece) that was found in the grave of a Hallstatt woman in France. Along with this ridiculously expensive and valuable item, she was buried with what was typical for women: tweezers, ear picks, combs, and jewelry. However, this particular woman, dubbed the Lady of Vix since Vix is the name of the site, also had numerous figures of dogs and young girls buried with her. These were molded and carved from expensive materials like glass and bronze and more ordinary materials like clay and jet. We do not know their purpose.

Gorgon head decorates a krater (huge urn) found at the Vix Grave.
WikiRigaou, CC BY-SA 4.0 <https://creativecommons.org/licenses/by-sa/4.0>, via Wikimedia Commons; https://commons.wikimedia.org/wiki/File:Vix_krater.jpg

The Lady of Vix is not the only example of an ancient Celtic woman receiving a lavish burial; it is simply the most famous. Without the misogynistic and imperial lens of the past and by donning more objective glasses and using the modern instruments they have on hand, archaeologists can say with confidence that Celtic women were largely honored upon their deaths, which leads us to believe they did enjoy a higher status than their contemporaries.

Basic Celtic Beliefs

The Celts were first bound together over vast territories and history through their language, but the next binding factor was their religious beliefs. It is difficult to describe a centralized Celtic belief system; rather, Celtic peoples throughout the ages, including today, have similar beliefs that bind them together.

One of the most central beliefs of the Celts was the sanctity of places in nature like holy groves and clear, fresh springs. Certain groves of trees were considered sacred because they were thought to be the dwelling places of the gods, often the goddess Nemetona. Once these sacred groves were found and ceremonially cleansed, they were blocked off on four sides to mark them as sacred places.

One religious belief that those of us reading this today might find intense is the importance the Celts placed on the human head, which was said to be the seat of the soul. That idea on its own may not be so astonishing, but from it sprung practices that may seem questionable through our modern eyes. Roman writers say the Celts worshiped the skulls of their ancestors, but a more likely practice was the embalming and preserving of enemies' heads after victory in battle. Preserving the heads and skulls of conquered foes is much more likely than cutting off the heads of beloved ancestors.

The Druids: An Introduction

Some people today claim to practice the Druidic religion, but it is simply a modern interpretation of what the ancient Celtic Druids did during the height of their religious power and prominence. The bottom line is we do not know much for sure about the ancient Celtic religious system, especially before the Celts moved westward and settled in Britain and Ireland. There is no centralized piece of Celtic writing that survives. In fact, the Druids, the leaders of society as chieftains, were so secretive that their body of beliefs, rituals, practices, and herbal knowledge was passed onto their acolytes orally.

The word "Druid" is shrouded in mystery. Even today, we are not sure why the Celtic judges, chieftains, medicine men and women, priests, teachers, and any other position of learning are referred to as "Druids." The name is attributed to the Celtic root meaning "to know" since the Druids were the most learned level of Celtic society.

However, unlike many of the people groups we refer to today, the Druids likely did call themselves something that sounded like that name. There is a Welsh term that refers to prophets as *dryw*, which has a similar pronunciation. Female Druids in Irish mythology were known as *ban-druí*.

The main idea behind introducing the Druids here is that as the Celts (whom the Romans referred to as Gauls) made their way west over the centuries (at the end of the Iron Age and into what we call the Classical Era), the Druids were the knowledge holders, the secret keepers, and the storytellers. Even today, we have a certain idea of mystical rituals in the forest conducted underneath the full moon, nature worship, and even human sacrifice. The Druids were part of the highest layer of Celtic society, along with the Celtic nobles, but they made sure to keep most of their knowledge secret. What we think we know comes from Irish mythology (in every myth, after all, is some grain of truth), which was promulgated through the Emerald Isle and the medieval world well after the Celts were part of the Irish narrative.

A nineteenth-century depiction of a Druid.
https://commons.wikimedia.org/wiki/File:An_Arch_Druid_in_His_Judicial_Habit.jpg

Chapter 2: Celtic Arrival in Ireland

The people we are getting to know, the Celts, began arriving in Ireland around 500 BCE. It was not a sudden migration, nor was it marked by the mass exodus of people to one location. The Celtic migration to Ireland can be likened to a small trickle of people who sailed through a period of several hundred years. Some historians think that some Celts began coming to Ireland prior to 500 BCE—the common window is between 800 and 400 BCE, but this is a rather unestablished idea. The year 500 BCE is what is generally accepted as the approximate time Celtic people began to call Ireland their home.

It may seem strange that a people so far-reaching and spread out so as to cover areas of what is now France, Germany, Switzerland, Austria, Spain, Portugal, and even as far south as Turkey would simply stop at some islands they landed on. Why did the Celts not continue their westward expansion past Britain and Ireland? There are several factors that contributed to the Celts' expansion into Britain and Ireland and their settlement there, especially in Ireland.

One reason they could not continue westward was that seafaring technology did not yet exist in Europe to make such strenuous ocean voyages as would be required of sailors from Ireland to the Americas. Another reason is that about a millennium after the Celts arrived and settled in Ireland, the Romans put an end to any possibility of the Celtic culture expanding anywhere else.

Did the Celts Invade Ireland?

From our present-day perspective, at first glance, the Celtic expansion from western and central Europe may remind us of a conquest-hungry people like the Norsemen or the Normans, but the Celtic expansion of and settlement in Ireland was slow, gradual, and, on the whole, peaceful.

The Norsemen, or the Vikings as we commonly call them, invaded England violently in the late 8th century CE, which was long after the arrival of the Celts in Ireland. There are marked differences between these two people groups arriving on the soil of Britain and Ireland (the Norsemen also conquered Ireland, famously naming Dublin from the words of their own language, meaning "black pool"). "Viking" is actually a profession, which is why the invaders are known as Vikings. The Scandinavians who rapidly and violently made it to Britain and other parts of Europe are actually called Norsemen (a distortion of "Northmen"). Viking is a title like sailor, farmer, or soothsayer.

Contrary to the bombastic and bloody Norse invasion of lands in Europe, the Celts more or less slowly settled in Ireland and made it their primary home base. After all, it's easier to feel at home in a land where you can build a culture, a society, a life, and shared history without being threatened on all sides by hungry empires (like the Greeks, the Romans, and even the Scythians at times).

The Normans would also come to call Britain their home, but that happened over two hundred years after the Norsemen invaded England at the hands of William the Conqueror, which happened in 1066. Both the Norsemen and the Normans came to forcefully take land, turn the locals into slaves and subjects, and rule the land on their terms. Sometimes, there were negotiations, but on the whole, the arrival of these two bloodthirsty groups centuries after the Celts' arrival on Irish soil spelled death and destruction for those inhabiting the islands, including the Celtic peoples themselves.

However, the Celts who settled in Ireland and Britain did so unassumingly, integrating themselves into the system that was already in place or finding land that was uninhabited to make their own. These Irish Celts are the ones we think about today when we discuss the ancient Celtic people and culture.

The Celts' arrival in Ireland allowed them to build a stronger cultural connection between tribes and chiefdoms. They never fully centralized but realized that allies were better than enemies, especially with the ever-looming Romans across a short stretch of water.

Travel and Trade

Just like the proto-Celtic cultures before them, the Irish Celts essentially insinuated themselves into existing Irish society, eventually becoming the dominant culture from about two hundred years after their initial arrival all the way to about 400 CE. The Gauls and Celts (the overlap on the European continent was such that there were almost no distinguishing features of the two peoples until the Celts left for Ireland, with the Gauls living in modern-day France under Roman occupation) always prospered because of alliances and trade. This was no different once the Celts reached Ireland.

The Celts brought iron tools to Ireland and the knowledge of how to forge and use them. Although most of the tools were farming and cooking implements, there were definitely weapons among those items the Celts introduced to the people already living in Ireland.

When the Celts arrived in Ireland, they were likely seeking new trading posts at first, but they eventually began to settle. One can go to Ireland today and see why the Celts were enchanted with the verdant green, lush landscape. They themselves contributed heavily to the Irish language and culture that we know and love today.

What probably began as reconnaissance for a trade mission allowed the migrating Celts to forge more alliances westward, ending up as a sort of homecoming for the ancient Celts.

Who were the people already inhabiting Ireland when the Celts arrived? We don't actually know a whole lot about them. We do know that the Celts did encounter Irish inhabitants because of gravesites and remnants of ancient villages. We do not know much else because although the Celts did develop a writing system, *ogham*, there are no surviving written records about with whom the Celts traded.

Written Language System

Although it is likely that the *ogham* language was inscribed upon perishable items like cloth and wood, the surviving examples of *ogham* are carved into stone monuments. The majority of these surviving examples represent personal names. The reason for this assumption is that several sounds of the language are missing from the stone monuments, although they were obviously used and survived. Therefore, there were likely plentiful Celtic writings in *ogham* that were too fragile to have survived throughout such a long time.

However, there are other theories about how *ogham* writing came to be used by the Celts in Ireland. Because *ogham* more than slightly resembles what we refer to as the Germanic runic alphabet (in popular culture, these are the "Viking runes," like in Tolkien's maps and metalheads' tattoos), anthropologists, linguists, and historians have suggested that perhaps *ogham* is simply a copy of Germanic runes. Because the Germanic runic alphabet does have those sounds missing from the surviving written examples of *ogham*, this theory explains that the sounds never disappeared at all.

Another theory is that *ogham* is simply a transliteration of the Latin alphabet, although Celtic consonants like /z/ and /w/ do not exist in the Latin alphabet. The reason this theory has any traction at all is that we know there was heavy contact between the Romans and the people of Britain, especially when these *ogham* monuments would have been inscribed.

Ogham monuments in Dunloe, Ireland.
Berthold Strucken, CC BY-SA 4.0 <https://creativecommons.org/licenses/by-sa/4.0>, via Wikimedia Commons; https://commons.wikimedia.org/wiki/File:Dunloe_(Ogham_Stones).jpg

Since the discovery (or perhaps recovery) of this system, there have been countless theories put forward about its origins, including the two mentioned above. It is important to note that the word *ogham* only refers to the writing method—the act of using a blade to carve into a hard surface. The group of letters themselves is known as the *Beith-luis-nin*, which is like saying "alphabet" (alpha and beta being the first letters of the Greek alphabet). *Beith-luis-nin* gets its name after the first three letters in the writing system.

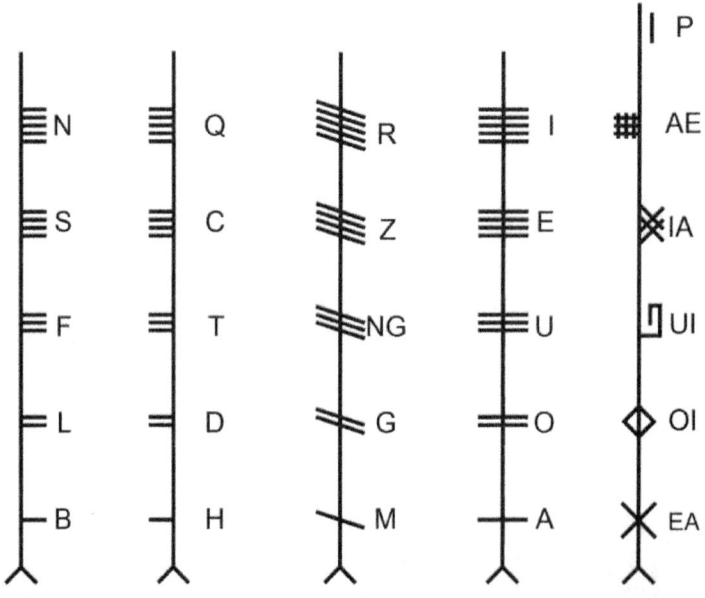

Ogham alphabet.
Runologe, CC BY-SA 4.0 <https://creativecommons.org/licenses/by-sa/4.0>, via Wikimedia Commons; https://commons.wikimedia.org/wiki/File:All_Ogham_letters_including_Forfeda_-_%C3%9Cbersicht_aller_Ogham-Zeichen_einschlie%C3%9Flich_Forfeda.jpg

Unfortunately, there is so much more that we don't know about Celtic writing and *ogham* than what we do know. Much like the disappearance of the English colonists at Roanoke, Virginia, and the location of the Ark of the Covenant, the Celts still hold many secrets, even after all these centuries.

Life after Arriving in Ireland

Despite what was to come, the Celts were relatively unmolested by the encroaching Romans, and for the most part, they did get along with other tribal peoples of Europe, such as the vast Germanic tribes and the

Gallic peoples (who were a Celtic group but developed a more separate identity than the Irish Celts). However, this does not mean the Celts did not know how to fight. They were fierce warriors who put their metalworking skills to the test by creating helmets, greaves, gauntlets, spears, and swords for battle. They saw the wisdom in nonviolence, but they could defend their families, farms, homes, and villages if necessary.

Most Celts were farmers, and they supplemented their crops by hunting wild game in Ireland's lush forests. They grew corn, barley, and rye, but eventually, wheat overtook all of these in prominence. When it came to hunting, wild boar was a staple, but venison was also hugely popular. The Celts also hunted foxes, beavers, and even bears. A bear provided fat for helping wounds heal, fur for clothing and bedding, and meat for an entire village.

To cook these morsels, the Celts used a cooking method in which they dropped heated stones into a large pot to make water boil. They added meat, vegetables, and herbs to this mixture, which was all cooked with stones. They kept the fire for the stones extremely hot so that they would always have a way to keep the water boiling.

Celtic Influence on Irish Culture

As we've mentioned above, very little is known about the inhabitants of Ireland before the Celtics came to have a major presence on the island. However, we do know the language that eventually developed into Irish Gaelic (still taught in Ireland today) came from a mixture of several Celtic languages and indigenous Irish tongues. As the Celts developed into a more Irish and less nomadic people, they adopted Irish Gaelic as their uniting tongue.

Although very little is known about the indigenous inhabitants of Ireland before the Celts, it is said that they had been there about seven or eight thousand years before the Celts first arrived. Ireland's topography is not the best for preserving organic materials (except in peat bogs), so not much is understood about the culture that reigned in Ireland before the Celts. There was a Bronze Age people called the Beakers, so-called for their style of beaker-shaped pottery, which does survive today. They may have shown the early Irish how to work with bronze, and they perhaps taught the Celts the same.

However, because the Celts were a major Iron Age culture in their own right, many artifacts and archaeological sites remain from their civilization. Besides the language evolution, which can still be seen and studied today, the Celts brought a unique sense of artwork, craftmanship, mythology, and even fighting methods, all of which are renowned today. The Celtic peoples who settled in Ireland more than 2,500 years ago are the ancestors of most of the Irish population, and so whatever indigenous groups preceded them have faded into history. In fact, the DNA of modern Irish people is mostly Celtic/Gaelic; this also includes the population of Northern Ireland. Irish Travellers (Romani) are the exception, but they were genetically similar until around the 1600s.

Essentially what we know is that early Irish culture influenced the Celts by providing linguistic characteristics that became Irish Gaelic, but all in all, the Celts *did* become an Irish culture a few hundred years after their arrival on Irish soil.

Chapter 3: Daily Life in Celtic Ireland

Farming

Most inhabitants of Ireland during the Bronze Age were farmers. The Iron Age, which followed, was really no different. These metal alloys could be used to create farming implements, which made it easier to complete more work in less time. Farmers could not only feed just their families but also trade surplus crops to purchase more farm implements or livestock or add on to their houses. Sometimes, crop surpluses were even used to purchase slaves.

Farming in Celtic Ireland during this time was virtually the same as it was in Britain. These methods remained the same for centuries. The Celts began to organize plots of farmland into regular rectangular shapes, and they would grow different crops on these plots and use some for animal grazing and some for cultivating hay. The animals the Celts raised normally slept indoors at night, either in a precursor to a small barn or under the family roof. Celts grew barley, corn, wheat, different types of beans, parsnips, spinach, carrots, garlic, and grains for animal feed (rye, millet, and spelt). They eventually grew flax to make textiles.

Farming Implements

Prior to using metal tools to speed up the farming process, the Celts (and everyone else) made farming tools, like hoes, rakes, and sickles, from animal bones. These tools were effective for a while, but they dulled faster and more easily than metal. Metal tools allowed the Bronze and Iron Age peoples to work faster and more efficiently, as they didn't have to replace their tools constantly. The plowshares farmers used were made of iron, but humans were still the muscle behind tilling the soil; animals were yet to be used as beasts of burden.

In order to acquire farmland in the first place, the Celts had to chop down and clear parts of forests or even huge swathes of trees they encountered in their new land. Since forests were considered a sacred part of their culture and belief system, they did not level all the land, but they still had to make room to cultivate their crops and pasture their animals. The most recognizable Celtic tool today and back then was the axe. Because the heads could be made of bronze or iron instead of stone or bone, felling trees had never been easier. The Celts then used some of the lumber to demarcate their different small fields for farming.

The Celts are known for their mobile colter, which simply yet ingeniously allowed farmers to plow and till their fields at the same time. The colter, a sharp, blade-like tool at the end of the plowshare, cut the soil vertically while the plow itself turned the cut soil with its horizontal bar. This type of colter and plowshare combination was in use for centuries because of its efficiency.

Another amazing Celtic farming invention was the wheeled plow. When we think of ancient peoples plowing and tilling the soil by hand, we often think of the Roman model, which was light enough for a person to carry and push laboriously through the soil. The Celts invented a heavier model, but it was supported on either side by a wheel, which made the extra weight insignificant to the worker but great for churning the soil.

Farming Techniques

Depleting the soil of nutrients has always been an issue ever since farming was invented around twelve thousand years ago. Through the millennia, farmers have been (and still are) discovering new and better ways to grow food and other crops. British and Celtic farmers learned that if the soil was being depleted, they could fertilize the fields with deep chalk pits and loam. Loam is part of the topsoil, and it is made up, depending on where it is found, of various percentages of silt, clay, and sand, meaning that it is found near water or where sources of water used to be. Loam provides much-needed nutrients to the soil, and chalk raises the pH level of the soil. Of course, the ancient Celts had no idea what a pH level was, but certain crops, such as beans, spinach, kale, and asparagus, grow very well in alkaline soils.

When Celtic farmers had a grain surplus, they would use granaries to store the extra produce. Most of these were built underground. Before the farmers would fill them up with dried grain, they would usually place an offering of some sort to the gods at the bottom of the granary.

Animal Husbandry

The Celts kept herds of cattle, from which they procured meat, milk, and clothing. They also kept some form of domesticated pig whose species no longer exists, and they raised sheep for their wool and goats for their milk—both of those were also consumed.

In fact, the Celts kept all the standard farm animals we think of today—chickens, geese, and even rabbits, although those probably more closely resembled wild hares than our fluffy bunnies of today. It has been speculated that the Celts used roosters for gaming cocks, as small, roofless enclosures have been found at their settlements that hardly differ from cock cages used today.

Julius Caesar, perhaps mistakenly, thought the Celts only kept fowl as pets, not for consumption. He made connections between the animals and certain speculated Celtic gods and goddesses, but we must remember that Greek and Roman outside observers were continually wrong about those whom they wrote about. More than likely, the Celts ate all the animals they kept.

Naturally, granaries would attract mice, so it is likely the Celts had close relationships with cats. Arguably, cats domesticated themselves—they are opportunists that realized life alongside humans would offer them food security and shelter. Dogs were used for hunting and were huge parts of Celtic heroic epics, as the hero typically had a canine companion of some sort.

Housebuilding

Like other Bronze Age societies in Europe, the main building method for houses and smaller structures (like roofed animal pens) was the wattle and daub method. This method primarily used wooden posts and bendable sticks collected from nearby woodlands. These posts and sticks would then be woven together like a huge basket. The Celts pounded the posts into the ground for stability, although they sometimes had to dig holes to get started, depending on how hard the ground was.

They then arranged the posts in a circle as large as they wished the home or structure to be. They would weave the twigs and sticks into something skinnier than the main skeletal poles; it was as if their home were a stable basket.

In order to fill the gaps between the weaves, a mixture of mud, clay, and even animal dung was used. Housebuilders made a mixture of these materials to "daub" onto the "wattle" that the house was constructed from. The mud, clay, and dung mixture would harden incredibly, although it did need repairs from time to time, especially after periods of inclement weather.

The floor was flat and made from packed earth. Eventually, this packed earth would become hard and strong after generations of feet walking over it and people sleeping on it. The roofs of these round, rather humble dwellings were thatched. This meant that people would need to dry straw and gather more twigs to layer on top of each other. They then bound these straw and twig bundles together in layers, making the roof waterproof. Some houses had small holes at the top for smoke to escape. Other families preferred not to get wet when it rained, so they made vents in their thatched roofs to allow smoke to escape. They didn't want to have to keep away from the middle of the house every time the sky opened up.

On the issue of privacy, there really wasn't much. Most of these round houses with thatched roofs had one room in which the family did everything: cooking, eating, making and repairing clothing, and watching children. Otherwise, activities were done outside unless it was extremely cold.

It might be surprising to think of whole families, often multi-generational, spending time inside a small one-room house together for hours on end. However, Bronze Age societies were very communal and different from what we are used to today, even for things like growing the family. It is likely that the couple was simply separated from other sleepers by just a curtain. The family would keep warm and chat around the fire, and as we mentioned earlier, they would use the hot stone method to cook stew. Rather than directly hanging a pot over the fire, Celtic chefs would place stones into a yellow-hot fire and then let those stones get hot enough to boil the water of the stew. If the temperature of the meal ran low, they would just add another stone. The Celts also roasted whole carcasses on spits over a fire.

Hunting, Fishing, and Foraging

Although the Celts were prolific farmers, they never stopped hunting wild game. The most popular animals to hunt in the woodlands were deer and wild boar. The Celts' favorite roasted meat was wild boar, which was even better than the domestic pigs they raised. The Celts sometimes consumed bear meat as well. It is unclear whether they purposely hunted bears to consume or whether these kills resulted as an act of self-defense.

The Celts also ate foxes and beavers. These animals were plentiful and, in the eyes of the Celts, edible and useful for their furs, so they were fair game, so to speak. Celts did not hunt on horseback; rather, they used hunting dogs to stalk prey like foxes or deer. They also sometimes split into two groups, with one group of hunters chasing their prey into the waiting spears of the other group. The Celts always hunted on foot, but since they did not hunt alone, they could look out for each other, warning against incoming dangers like the errant bear or irate boar. Typically, spears were the weapons of choice when hunting and fishing.

It's only natural that Celtic settlements developed near freshwater sources, which were typically rivers but sometimes large lakes. This means that a large part of their diet came from fatty freshwater fish, such as salmon, trout, and mackerel. These fish provided much-needed omega-3 fatty acids and vitamin C to the Celts. The Celts also often ate eels. Celtic people caught fish typically one at a time by using spears, but they also developed trapping methods just like ancient societies all over the world. They wove baskets for fish to swim into but could not escape. This was a labor-saving way of catching fish while performing other duties.

The Celts supplemented their meat, fish, and grain diet with sweet things too. They foraged for fruits (not necessarily cultivating them themselves until much later) like many types of berries, including blackberries, gooseberries, and blueberries. They also foraged for mushrooms, ate eggs of wild birds, and apples they could reach or that fell from trees. They even consumed nettles, which can be prickly and dangerous to the touch. Nettles were likely used for medicinal purposes.

Although other societies much older than the Celts, like the ancient Egyptians, Greeks, and some Middle Eastern societies, managed to keep/domesticate bees in manmade beehives, the Celts foraged for honey. Beeswax has always been useful and highly prized, as has honey for its delicious sweetness and medicinal properties. As far as we know, Celts did not keep bees domestically, but they still benefited from their hard work by consuming honey and using beeswax.

A Day in the Life

Now that we've discussed the typical arrangements of diet and housing, what did a normal day look like for a Celtic peasant? Noblemen and noblewomen had household staff and were too busy deciding on the future of the settlement, so let's take a look at what a typical day would look like for a peasant girl in a Bronze Age Celtic village.

- If you were a peasant girl in the Bronze Age, you would first get water from a well or from the river for your morning tasks, like cooking and freshening up. This would also be for your family to use as well.
- Breakfast might consist of some leftover stew from the night before, some fruit, some bread, or even some fresh milk from cows or goats.
- Chances are that even though you're a girl, you and your brothers all know how to make tools from flint and animal bones. You would likely get started for the day by sharpening your bone needles and mending clothing or blankets or perhaps continuing your work tanning animal hides from the day before.
- Feeding the animals is hugely important. The pigs get the scraps, and the cows and sheep are usually fine on their own, although they would appreciate some hay or straw. Chickens can feed on corn and other seeds you give them.
- Lunch likely consists of a meat stew boiled with vegetables, but perhaps you and your family went with salted pork, venison, or fish to sustain you in the middle of your day.
- If it happens to be harvest time, you and your whole family are in the fields harvesting crops that are ready to be used or traded

as surplus. It's rough work, but luckily, you had that stew for lunch.

- By the late afternoon or evening, the animals need to be fed again, and the ones in the field need to be brought in from the pasture. Your assistance is probably needed with this.

- Dinner is already roasting over the fire indoors on a spit. Your younger siblings are playing with stick men they've made, making them fierce warriors with spears going after a wild boar. You rinse off with a wet rag before sitting around the fire, and you and your family talk about the different tasks of the day and what you all plan to do with your crops. The roast is done, and everyone eats with their hands, savoring the greasy deliciousness of the meat.

- Once everyone is full, the carcass is buried, and it's time to sleep. You curl up on your pile of blankets and furs that you likely share with your siblings, and then you drift off into a deep sleep, your mind and body craving the rest. It's still early for us modern folks with electricity, but you get up with the sun and labor all day. It's best to sleep early to have enough energy to do it all again.

Celtic Crafters

Apart from being capable hunters, fishers, gatherers, and, most importantly, farmers and animal domesticators, we cannot overlook the Celtic propensity for creating art and even imbuing ordinary objects with gorgeous decorations. The Celts made intricate personal decorations, such as brooches, which they used to hold their cloaks around their shoulders. They also made collars called torcs, like the Broighter Collar. It is the most famous example of Irish goldsmithing in the Irish/Celtic style during the Bronze Age.

Golden Broighter collar (torc).
Sailko, CC BY 3.0 <https://creativecommons.org/licenses/by/3.0>, via Wikimedia Commons; https://commons.wikimedia.org/wiki/File:Tesoro_di_oggetti_d%27oro_di_broighter,_contea_di_derry,_I_secolo_ac,_bracciale_con_viticci.jpg

The Celts also made ordinary items extraordinary by giving them that extra artistic touch. Spears and swords were engraved with swirling designs and sometimes animals like deer, wolves, bears, and foxes. The handles of swords were also inlaid with semi-precious stones or materials like bone, ivory, and amber and were often intricately carved as well. There are several examples of these painstakingly carved handles on heavy Celtic swords. These featured a human form, and the torso was where the wielder placed their grip, with the arms and legs of the human helping to stabilize the sword during battle. The Celts had a special veneration for the human head (which the Greeks and Romans emphasized in strange ways that may or may not be the truth), and the pommel of the sword was sometimes made into a human head shape. Many of these human head pommels wore fearsome and grotesque expressions, but some were more neutral and blander. It probably depended on what the warrior preferred when commissioning a sword.

Celtic swords were decorated lovingly, but so were their scabbards (the sheath of a sharp weapon). The whole surface could be decorated. Since scabbards were made of a softer material than iron or bronze, like leather or wood, they offered an easier medium to work with when making intricate designs. Swirling and twisting dragons were popular motifs and found on many scabbards. Other popular designs included climbing and curling flowering vines, some of these including animal figures hidden throughout or famous scenes from Celtic mythology.

Horses eventually became extremely important to the Celts, and they would also use them to pull war chariots. As such, horse bridles, saddles, chariot rings, reins, and any other horse-related paraphernalia were decorated for the chieftains and high-ranking Celtic warriors who commissioned them. Designs that adorned these horses and their kits were spirals and knots, the aforementioned floral patterns, and sometimes scenes of a battle.

Gold was an extremely popular material for jewelry, torcs, lock rings (devices used to hold hair back), brooches, and even fancy horse tack for chieftains.

The Celtic artistic style was also evident in woven textiles and even in tools. The Celts decorated their tools, with they then used to decorate other things in their homes. There is something intriguing about making an ordinary item beautiful, whether it is for a spiritual purpose, marking possession, or simply for the sake of beauty.

PART TWO:
Myth, Folklore, and Religion

Chapter 4: Pagan Gods and Goddesses

No material on the Celts would be incomplete without coverage of their pantheon of fascinating gods and goddesses. These entities played hugely important roles in the lives of ordinary Celts as they went about their days, interacted with nature, and created implements invoking good luck or reverence to these deities.

The decision-makers, the noble people, and the Druids were even more influenced by this powerful pantheon. Many noble families insisted that their lineage traced back to the supernatural race to which the gods and goddesses belong, the Tuatha Dé Danann—more about them later on. Let's take a look at the most important and interesting deities that make up the main players of Celtic belief and mysticism.

The Dagda

The Dagda is the patriarch of the Celtic pantheon. He is similar to the Norse god Odin in that he is responsible for fathering many, being the god of wisdom, and carrying a staff. But this is where the similarities between the two end.

The Dagda is a typically even-tempered god with an easy-going sense of humor. Humans can joke at his expense, and his mercy allows him to appreciate the joke and not seek vengeance. Epithets for the Dagda used by the Celts include words and phrases that roughly convey the following meanings: the great god, the fertile one, the great father, the all-father, and the lord of great knowledge.

Several powerful objects are associated with the Dagda besides his beard and long, flowing cloak, which are the only defining characteristics of his appearance, along with his enormous size. The most important objects the Dagda possesses are his staff, his cauldron, and his harp.

With the staff, which is extremely long, he can kill many men with just the outer side. But if the Dagda so chooses, he can raise the dead with the inner end of the staff. He literally holds the power of life and death in his hands. The staff is the main reason the Dagda is so powerful and can drive off the Fomorians, a mythological race of ragtag magical creatures that the Druids believed inhabited Ireland before their gods defeated them. It is actually unclear because of translation challenges whether the Dagda actually wields a staff, a club, or a mace. Scholars of Celtic lore all agree that it holds the power of death and life and that it is a weapon matching the size of the Dagda.

The second artifact the Dagda is known to have is a cauldron nicknamed "the un-dry cauldron" since it is always full. No one will walk away with an empty stomach after eating from that cauldron—it is bottomless, and not only that, but it can hold a dozen humans, with the ladle itself comfortably able to fit two inside. The cauldron can be seen as a symbol of the Dagda's rule over agriculture and the seasons. The cauldron never went empty, and so it can be extrapolated from that idea that his wish for the Celts was that there would not be famine but always plenty.

How did the Dagda control the changing of the seasons? He had a harp that was made of oak that he used to keep the seasons in their proper time. Some legends say that the harp stirred men's hearts so that they would be courageous while plunging into battles. The Dagda also had fruit trees that always produced.

Where could one find the Dagda, his power and wisdom, and all this bounty? Newgrange is a Stone Age tomb located in the east of Ireland. This monument, which still hosts a few hundred thousand visitors annually, is said to be the home of the Dagda. It was designed so that at the winter solstice, sunlight shines through the hole built into the roof and illuminates its passageways. It has been a site of pagan significance and worship for more than five thousand years.

The Cailleach

The Cailleach is also simply known as the Hag, and she is the goddess of winter. It is unsurprising that a place with such damp, gloomy, and sometimes prolonged winters as Ireland has its own goddess for that particular season.

The Cailleach.
No restrictions;
https://commons.wikimedia.org/wiki/File:Wonder_tales_from_Scottish_myth_and_legend_(1917)_(14566397697).jpg

Her rule over the winter season begins right after the end of what we now know as Halloween, October 31st, which the Celts started and still call Samhain. The Cailleach actually controls how long the winter is, which is why it was so important for the Celts to stay on her good side. If anything was displeasing to the winter hag, she could make the winds blow harsh and loud over the land and plunge them into a deeper and longer winter.

Despite the fact that she is nicknamed the Hag and has quite an alarming appearance, like the Dagda, she is depicted as a personality on the neutral side of the spectrum; she is neither good nor evil. Those attributes are usually kept for lesser deities, mystical creatures, and humans. The Cailleach has one eye and extremely pale skin, the color of snow, but she is extremely powerful, despite having an odd limping way of leaping and scaling the landscape. She can even carve out valleys and create mountains. This description makes her seem a giantess, the size of even the Dagda. Boulders and landslides can slip right out of her apron, where she holds these structures.

The most important aspect of Cailleach's appearance is her veil. In fact, in Irish and Scottish Gaelic today, her name literally means "hag." However, the etymology of the term is much older, originally meaning "veiled one." The Cailleach is, in fact, also known as the Veiled One and the more flattering Queen of Winter. The ancient Gaelic meaning of "veiled one" is said to have originated from the Latin root *pallium*, meaning woolen cloak.

Like the Dagda, the Cailleach also has a staff, although this one lacks the power to grant instant life and resurrection. It freezes the ground or whatever it touches. In the Scottish tradition, she also carries a hammer for smashing and shaping the landscape. The Cailleach does not have horns herself, as the Dagda sometimes does, but she has control over deer and other horned animals. She herds them and even cares for them during the harsh winter months. This is what cements her as perhaps the second most important deity in the Celtic pantheon. The Dagda is called the father of the gods, and the Cailleach is considered the mother.

The home of the Cailleach is said to be on or near the Beara Peninsula in southern Ireland.

As the Cailleach controls winter, she works together with the goddess Brigid, who rules over the summer. Some legends have it that they are one and the same, with the Cailleach turning her face and Brigid taking over when winter is over and vice versa. Some other legends liken the Cailleach to a much more inhuman deity than Brigid and say she turns to stone each year when her job is finished, allowing the humanoid (and much more aesthetically pleasing) Brigid to rule over the warmer seasons.

Brigid

The Cailleach rules over the winter, and Brigid rules over the summer. Brigid is the daughter of the Dagda, and there is some fuzziness over whether Brigid (or Brigit or Bríg) was one goddess or a triune goddess; however, most of the literature and oral traditions passed down say that this Brigid, the goddess of summer, was also the goddess of wisdom, poets, and protection. Her two sisters, also called Brigid, were called Brigid the physician or healer and Brigid the smith. This is why she is sometimes considered a triune or tripartite goddess, which would be one entity with three different functions.

Brigid, depicted in 1917.
https://commons.wikimedia.org/wiki/File:Thecomingofbrideduncan1917.jpg

However, later literature written by Christians in Ireland suggests that "Brigit" was a title for a goddess, so Brigid may very well have been three separate sisters.

As the Cailleach's season is welcomed at the close of Samhain, the season of Brigid is ushered in at Imbolc on February 1st each year. This is when the Hag lays down her staff and, in many legends, turns to stone until the next Samhain. It is now Brigid's turn to take over.

Brigid's main duties include healing, protection, and looking after domesticated animals. While the Cailleach cares for deer and wild animals, looking after livestock as well during the winter months, Brigid acts as a shepherd for the Celts' domesticated livestock, alerting them if there are any illnesses spreading among them and keeping herds together.

When she is merged together with her two sisters as one entity, she becomes the goddess of healing and smithing, which makes her quite a talented individual. Brigid is associated with spring because Imbolc, which is her annual celebration, venerates fertility and is traditionally the start of the season when ewes begin to give birth. As the patroness of domesticated animals and fertility, Brigid is very busy during the spring months.

Any section about the goddess Brigid would be incomplete without the mention of St. Brigid of Kildare, which the Catholics merged with the Celtic goddess Brigid. There is still some friction between the Catholic and pagan communities, the latter of which still celebrate February 1st as Imbolc rather than the feast day of St. Brigid.

The Morrigan

The Morrigan is another Celtic deity that may actually be three separate goddesses or a single deity with three facets or main aspects. The Morrigan can be compared to the Greek god Ares, the god of war. She meddles and stirs up men's hearts, which then leads to conflict, battles, and ultimately death. She is known as the goddess of war and death. However, because the Morrigan is the Dagda's husband, and they are both powerful warrior deities, their coupling is celebrated on Samhain when the Cailleach is welcomed.

The Morrigan has the power to shapeshift into any living being, including beautiful and terrifying humans, fish, birds, mammals, or even the wind, which, according to the Celts, was arguably living. Her typical appearance is meant to inspire terror and awe, as she is the goddess of war and death. However, she can choose to appear how she wishes to whoever views her, be that as a wolf, a raven, a young woman, a hideous hag, or something else altogether. According to the Táin Bó Regamna, a story that recounts a cattle raid and is part of a whole genre of much later Celtic tales that were written down, describes the Morrigan as a red-haired woman with a red cloak, bringing to mind Melisandre from *Game of Thrones*.

No depictions of the Morrigan survive from the time of her heyday, which, if the terrifying descriptions are anything to go by, might be for the best. Since she can appear any way she chooses, does she really have a true form in the first place?

The Morrigan and the Dagda are the true definition of a power couple, and they had several children together, including Brigid. They have three sons: Aengus, Cermait, and Aed, and another daughter, Bodb Derg. However, just because they are married does not mean that the Dagda and the Morrigan are faithful to each other. The Morrigan had children with others, and she famously attempted to seduce one of the most famous Celtic heroes, Cú Chulainn, but failed.

Legend says that the Dagda wondered how best to win a battle once upon a time, a time that would eventually come to be celebrated as Samhain. There was a woman bathing in the Unis River in Connacht, which was not far from his home, especially if he was a giant. She was comely, and he was smitten pretty much immediately. The woman told him how to win his battle. He married her, and that woman, the Morrigan, and the Dagda predicted how well the harvest would go each Samhain by performing their marital duties.

This is an interesting juxtaposition—the Dagda is more awed than feared, although he does have control over almost every aspect of life and death. The Morrigan, on the other hand, is more complex yet has less control. She is the goddess of priestesses, spellcasting, divination, war, conflict, bloodshed, and violence. She does not have the power to resurrect, unlike her husband, the lord of agriculture, seasons, time, life, and rebirth.

Cernunnos

Cernunnos is a god from the Celtic religion that seems older and slightly more obscure than the ones we've already discussed. Essentially, his name means "the horned one," and he is known as the god of all wild things. He is often accompanied by a stag; Cernunnos has two horns himself.

Cernunnos.
Nationalmuseet, CC BY-SA 3.0 <https://creativecommons.org/licenses/by-sa/3.0>, via Wikimedia Commons; https://commons.wikimedia.org/wiki/File:Gundestrupkedlen-00054_(cropped).jpg

This may be confusing, as Brigid takes care of domesticated animals, and the Cailleach cares for animals as well, but Cernunnos does not have a period of inactivity during the year like the goddesses mentioned. He is active all year round.

Cernunnos prefers life with animals, away from humans, deep in the forest. Although Cernunnos seems obscure, he could be even older than the Dagda and the Morrigan, with representations of him in art found from Romania all the way to Ireland. In fact, by the time Christians arrived in Ireland, he had a cult that was going strong. It is not uncommon for people's devotion to particular gods and goddesses to wax and wane over time, and Cernunnos seems to be one of the original gods of the first Celts, as well as one of the more popular ones toward the end of Celtic dominance in Ireland.

He is associated with fertility, the forest, and flora and fauna. He can be likened to the Greek god Dionysus because of his love for the forest, but that is where the comparison abruptly ends. Cernunnos is not concerned with raucous moonlit celebrations in his honor, and he prefers the company of animals to humans. This does not mean that Cernunnos the horned one has not been venerated as much as he deserves—he is one of the most represented figures in Celtic art throughout the whole Bronze Age and the Iron Age. He is easily recognizable by his stag horns.

When Julius Caesar wrote about the "barbarian Celts," he compared Cernunnos to Dis Pater, the Roman father of Jupiter (Zeus). In this way, we can also see that Cernunnos is perhaps even older than the Dagda and is where the main pantheon of Celtic deities originates.

One interesting theory of where the idea of a horned devil in Christian tradition originated is with the Christian monks who came to Ireland. The cult of Cernunnos had been gaining traction for a while, and the Christians even called him the Antichrist and used his horned image as a representation of the devil (a monster with horns is a medieval construct for Lucifer—previously he was just a fallen angel). Several factors likely came together to vilify the Wild One of the Forest, and this is quite possibly a consequence of the slander.

Although Cernunnos is known today as an important Celtic deity due to the backlash from the Christians later on, as well as the persistent depictions of him throughout Celtic history on art pieces, it is possible that he never was a god in the first place. There is almost nothing written about him from Celtic sources. None of the surviving literature or art pieces identify the horned one as a god, so it is possible that this is a huge case of mistaken identity. Cernunnos could simply be a venerated shaman, a Druid with enormous power and wisdom with a cult of his own (including animal sacrifices and sometimes human ones) simply because of his own human achievements, which have been lost in the annals of time. This simply adds to the mystery of the Druids, the Celts, and their ancient pagan religion.

Lugh

Lugh is a god known for his mastery of athletic skills; in fact, one of his nicknames, Samildánach, literally means "equally good at all the skills/arts." The origin of his name, Lugh or Lug, is a confusing one, and no scholar can agree on its origin. Some say it comes from a root meaning "to swear a contract," while some say it comes from a root meaning "flashing light." The cases for each are weak at best—again, this simply adds to the mystery of Celtic theology that we may never discover.

Lugh is often depicted riding a horse and wielding a spear. He is famously good at, well, everything, but throwing spears is a special skill of his and one that he practices daily. Lugh is larger than a human, but he is not considered a giant like the Dagda. In one of the legends of famed Irish hero Cú Chulainn, Lugh is described as young-looking with curly blond hair and wearing a green cloak. Of course, he sits on a horse. He also carries a five-pointed spear and a javelin in the same hand.

Despite the lethality of Lugh's favorite weapons (indeed, these were the preferred hunting weapons of the Celts), he mostly makes games and contests with them rather than causing bloodshed.

Lugh is the son of the god Cian and the goddess Eithne, and this is notable because Eithne is the daughter of Balor. Balor is the ruler of the Fomorians, the nasty little beasts that inhabited Ireland before the deities, the Tuatha Dé Danann, kicked them out. Lugh ends up killing his grandfather Balor. Lugh is also mentioned in some legends as the father of Cú Chulainn, with Cú Chulainn's mother being a mortal woman. This would explain Cú Chulainn's strength, craftiness, cunning, and skill as a warrior, although we will mention that a little later.

Sometimes, Lugh is remembered as a trickster god, a little bit like the Norse god Loki. It is said that when thunderstorms occur, the lightning and thunder are Lugh and Balor battling.

Epona

Simply put, Epona is the goddess of horses. The Gallic (remember, Gallic and Irish Gaelic broke off from a larger Gaelic language group) root *epo-* means horse. The suffix *-ona* means on. She is literally "on a horse." It might seem silly to us for people to have a goddess fully dedicated to equines (horses, donkeys, and mules), but this makes perfect sense to a Stone and Bronze Age culture during a time when monumental developments in farming, herding, and warfare were being discovered and implemented in everyday life. The horse was central to Celtic life. Eventually, devotion to Epona reached all the way to Rome. The Roman Empire worshiped her, despite the fact that she was originally a Celtic goddess.

The goddess Epona with her horses.
Rosemania, CC BY 2.0 <https://creativecommons.org/licenses/by/2.0>, via Wikimedia Commons; https://commons.wikimedia.org/wiki/File:Epona.jpg

When Epona is depicted, she is typically accompanied by a horse or donkey with her hand resting on its head, seated regally next to the beast.

Epona was revered in Celtic villages, where families had a horse or two and a few donkeys to help with their labor and to check on their land. Epona was called upon when a mare was in labor to ensure the foal would be born healthy and so that the mare would recover swiftly.

Although she was a Celtic goddess, you have to remember that the Gauls and the Celts were one people at one time, and they remained closely related in language and culture. The Gauls relied heavily on their cult of Epona because of their fierce cavalry, which defeated the Roman conquerors time and time again. Thus, Epona became a patron goddess of military cavalries due to their reliance on their noble mounts. When the Romans eventually took over, they adopted Epona into their pantheon and renamed her Augusta.

Goibniu

Many Celtic gods and goddesses were warriors, and the number one thing they were always in need of was metal goods and repairs to their existing weapons. This is where Goibniu comes in. He is the god of metalsmithing, and as such, he was the patron god of human blacksmiths. More importantly, though, he was the smith to the Tuatha Dé Danann. The Celtic pantheon needed weapons, spears, equipment maintenance, and, of course, horseshoes.

Who better to outfit the gods and goddesses with their metal items than a god of smithing? Goibniu is also included in the trio of the gods of art, which also includes a silversmith and a carpenter. This trio was essential for the Tuatha Dé Danann to defeat the Fomorians (which we *will* cover, don't worry).

Apart from his absolutely crucial role as the smith of the gods, Goibniu is also known as a master brewer and for his legendary hospitality. As such, he was the patron god of tavern owners, brewers, and innkeepers. His skill for putting on feasts for the gods and goddesses earns him a drama-free place among the pantheon. One fun fact to make Goibniu even more interesting is that during a battle, one of Brigid's sons stabbed him with a spear. Goibniu simply removed the spear, stabbed Brigid's son with it, and killed him.

Ériu

Ériu's very name is the root of the name of the land of Ireland, which in modern Irish Gaelic is Éire. She is the embodiment of the land of Ireland. The mythical Milesians are said to be the humans who first inhabited Ireland and eventually became the Celts. We know this is all according to legend. Ireland did have normal human inhabitants before the Celts arrived; we just don't have much in the archaeological record to give us a robust picture of who those people really were.

However, according to Celtic mythology, the Tuatha Dé Danann inhabited Ireland before any humans did, and the Milesians were the ones who forced them underground. The gods and goddesses were still present and working, but they weren't the dominant inhabitants of the land. Like the Dagda, the gods and goddesses inhabited burial mounds, sacred groves, and other sites holy to the Celts rather than parading about on land like they did before the Milesians defeated them.

This is important because the last words of Ériu before she was driven underground with the rest of the Tuatha Dé Danann is that the land would be named after her. She scaled a hill called Uisneach, which is now the sacred center of Ireland to pagans. The hill is located in County Westmeath. At the Hill of Uisneach, Ériu demanded the

Milesians name the land after her, and it was so. It was known as Éire ever after.

Ériu is the goddess of fertility and abundance. The root of her name means abundance or bounty, which makes perfect sense, with the rolling green hills and fertile farmlands of Ireland lasting to this day. She is also known as the goddess of sovereignty since she was able to get the whole island country named after her. As such, she also has the responsibility and privilege to be the matron goddess of the land of Ireland itself.

Áine

Our last deity on this list deserves a place because she is one of the most revered goddesses in western Ireland. Several places are named after Áine all over County Limerick, including the Hill of Cnoc Áine and at least three other town names. Why is Áine so beloved? She is the goddess of warmth, fertility, and the sun. These three things were extremely important to ancient peoples, especially the Celts. Without these three aspects of the natural world, death would follow.

Midsummer celebrations at the solstice are carried out in Áine's honor, with the last recorded one openly occurring less than two hundred years ago. Áine is not only beloved for the characteristics she represents (abundant harvest, new growth, wealth, and prosperity) but also for her personality. She is said to have been raped by a king, but she bit off his ear so everyone would know what he had done. Many families in Ireland today have family lore that includes the goddess Áine as an ancestor.

Chapter 5: Traditional Celtic Festivals

Like many ancient cultures and traditions, the Celtic festivals and holidays followed the moon rather than the sun. The Gregorian calendar, which we use around the world today, was not adopted until the time of Shakespeare, which is why even as recently as the Middle Ages, specific dates of important events are often disputed (the Julian calendar was the solar calendar in use before the Gregorian calendar was adopted).

The Jews, Muslims, Chinese, and pagans still use the moon to dictate the dates of their important holidays, which means the dates of these festivals change each year. The Celts were no different. Although their feast days and traditional festivals were seasonally based, events like the winter or summer solstices do not fall on the same Gregorian date each year.

It must be stated that the modern celebrations of traditional Celtic festivals do have steady dates (Samhain on November 1st, Imbolc on February 1st, etc.) because of the Christianization of Ireland, as priests and missionaries attempted to be more appealing to the Celts by aligning All Saints' Day and St. Brigid's Feast Day with Samhain and Imbolc. Thus, these two have specific dates in the modern world.

However, since the ancient Celts did not mark time in the same way that we do, instead relying on the sun, the moon, the stars, and seasonal changes to mark a year, these important festivals would fall whenever a significant seasonal event occurred. And because these traditions were so ancient, and the Celts built monuments like Newgrange to mark solstices and equinoxes, they were able to track the year's movements and celebrate accordingly.

We will cover the four essential traditional Celtic festivals here, as well as four minor festivals. These were all important events to mark different aspects of what was happening in nature around the Celts, to honor their deities, and to garner favor for new seasons. The modern pagan community that identifies as modern practicing Druids and witches celebrate these holidays today, albeit much differently (there are fewer sacrifices, for one thing). There are eight main holidays in the wheel of the Celtic year, and an eight-spoked wheel, much like the one in Buddhism, is used by Neopagans to represent the yearly cycle. Let's get into how the ancient Celts celebrated these eight important holidays.

The Wheel of the Year.
https://commons.wikimedia.org/wiki/File:Wheel_of_the_Year.svg

Yule

Yule occurs with the arrival of the winter solstice. Because of the shortening of the days, it represented the rebirth of the sun (and whatever deities the people of the Stone and Bronze Ages associated with the sun) and was a portent hailing the return of new growth and springtime. It was not seen as a barren, empty time but a time of hope for new beginnings, a time for the sun to rest so that it could return in all its glory to revive the land and help all living things flourish.

Eventually, the associations with Yule, the winter solstice, changed. The Celts, no doubt helped along by their portrayal of the winter hag Cailleach, began to associate the beginning of winter with death and the harshness winter brings. They still celebrated Yule at Stone Age sites like Newgrange and Stonehenge, but the idea was more somber and less full of hope than it had been when celebrated in generations past.

If Yule sounds familiar, we sometimes use the term Yuletide to describe the arrival of Christmastime. The association of evergreen plants, holly and its berries, mistletoe, ivy, and wreaths come from this ancient holiday. The Celts made wreaths and bound sprigs of these winter plants together and gave them as offerings. They also used them as decorations for their homes. They also decorated trees—sound familiar?

In order to offset the bleakness of Midwinter, which is another name for Yule and the winter solstice, the Celts held many feasts in their own homes and in the homes of family and friends. They gave gifts as well. If this sounds like Christmas, it is pretty much the same, minus the tradition of hanging stockings. Also, today, we do not typically sacrifice animals to any deities during the Christmas season.

Imbolc (Spring)

This holiday, known in modern times as St. Brigid's Feast Day, aligns with North American Groundhog Day, which is celebrated a day later. Both symbolize the impending arrival of spring, which is how the association began. However, Imbolc is the original celebration of the goddess Brigid, and it is right between the winter solstice and the spring equinox.

Imbolc was celebrated to usher in spring after the long winter. Although the weather may still resemble its icy wintry character, by welcoming in springtime on February 1st, the Celts were optimistically looking forward to warmer and more fertile times ahead. Since Brigid, daughter of the Dagda, is the goddess of wealth, prosperity, domesticated animals, and fertility, she is the perfect patroness for springtime. As we mentioned earlier, there are several different ways to tell the story, but Brigid has control of the light half of the year, taking the weather and season mantle from the Cailleach, who controls the dark half of the year.

Not much literature from the same time as ancient Celtic Imbolc practices survived, but a continuous theme is the pregnancy of ewes and the birth of lambs around this time. We have discussed how important sheep were for the Celts as sources of wool, meat, and sometimes milk. Since sheep give birth earlier in the year than cattle, the arrival of lambs was inextricably linked with the arrival of spring.

Ostara

Although Ostara takes place on the actual vernal equinox (the start of spring), Imbolc is the holiday associated with spring's actual arrival. Because the days began lengthening, Ostara was a celebration that those light days had arrived instead of just a symbol of hope for warmer times to come. Ostara typically arrived during what is now the third week of March on the Gregorian calendar, which would be the time when the green hills of Ireland and all its natural glory were on full display.

This holiday is not as ancient as the others, with records of its celebration appearing around the 8th century. It is a corrupted spelling of the name of the goddess Eostre, which some people say is where we get the name Easter (there are many etymological theories for the name Easter; this is simply the one that comes from Britain and Ireland). Eostre is a Germanic goddess representing spring. Since she is an import, it makes sense that her holiday is a later addition to the Celtic calendar. However, she is associated with rabbits and eggs, symbols of fertility.

Beltane (Summer)

Beltane normally falls on or around May 1st, and it falls between Ostara (the spring equinox) and Litha, one of the major Celtic solar festivals. Its celebration by Celts was largely influenced by Germanic tribes, with even some Roman influence thrown in. The Romans venerated the goddess Flora at the time, and this adoration carried over to Ireland. Instead of having a specific goddess by the name of Flora, the Celts celebrated the concept of fertility in general. Fertility was a key aspect of ancient life in all cultures, and the Celts were no exception.

Celebration and joy were on full display, filled with bonfires for purity. People danced and made music around the fires, encouraging and celebrating fertility. The reason bonfires were so important at Celtic festivals is that they represented the power of the sun, and the Celts believed that fire had cleansing properties. On Beltane, they would light two huge bonfires and walk their cattle between them, cleansing the cattle and ensuring they would produce plenty of milk and calves.

The modern iteration of this pagan holiday involves dancing around maypoles, donning flower crowns, and celebrating summer's arrival. It is known as May Day.

Litha

Litha, or the summer solstice, is the longest day of the year, and the sun is celebrated in all its power and magnificence. It is also called Midsummer and typically falls during the third week of June. The Celts absolutely loved their bonfires, and Litha was a special day for them. The Celts would light bonfires on top of hills so they could be seen for miles, and those daring enough on the summer solstice would attempt to leap through the fires to garner good luck. This seems like a steep price to pay for luck, but ancient peoples were nothing if not thorough when it came to ensuring prosperity.

Some legends say that because this is the longest day of the year, it is a battle between the light and the dark. After all, in ancient Celtic tradition, the year is split in two—the light half and the dark half. But, of course, inevitably, the dark side of the year wins; the longest day of the year eventually comes to a close, and the days shorten from Litha onward. There are records of celebrants lighting huge wheels on fire, then proceeding to roll (and even race) the enflamed wheels down hills to the shores of a nearby river. Fire and light reigned during Litha, which itself means "light."

Lughnasadh (Autumn)

Lughnasadh is one of three harvest festivals celebrated by pagans, but in the Celtic tradition, this festival more recently marked the beginning of the harvest season. This holiday is typically celebrated on August 1st, making it another "halfway holiday," this time in the middle of the summer solstice and the autumnal equinox. However, in ancient Celtic practice, Lughnasadh fell between harvest time and planting season, which means that the largely agricultural Celtic society was at a bit of a standstill. Hence, the festival of Lughnasadh was born.

As you may have surmised already, the festival contains the name of the god Lugh, the master of all skills. The Celts took this time of idleness between harvesting and planting to host games, bringing different villages and communities together for the competitions. These competitions were more ritualistic and religious in nature than they were for the sheer sport of it, from what little we know of them. Scholars believe they involved spear-throwing, perhaps arrow shooting, maybe hunting, and definitely fire in some form. The Celts were wonderful storytellers, and there is evidence that shows they would put on plays honoring Lugh and his defeat of the blight, which eliminates harvests.

These festivities usually took place in high places, such as plateaus or hilltops, which gave participants and spectators ample viewing for the role-playing exercises and the sacrifices, which typically included the first fruits of the village harvest and a bull.

This harvest festival was such a big deal that there were often corresponding traveling markets and fairs to sell and trade surplus crops and to prolong the festivities. Lughnasadh was definitely a festival where one could have a good time, and it took the people's minds off the fact that they could not yet plant new crops in this in-between time.

Mabon

The celebration of the autumnal equinox is a pagan harvest festival, the second of three. The name Mabon was not used until 1970, and the Celts probably did not celebrate this as a major holiday. We mention it here because it is included in the Wheel of the Year, and during the autumnal equinox, there is no doubt that the ancient Celts marked the occasion in some way. However, we do not think that it was a major, bonfire-lighting, feasting occasion. It was simply another way to mark the passing of the days and may have been lightly celebrated with fall fruits and a hearty meal.

Samhain (Winter)

Samhain was arguably the most important ancient Celtic festival. This holiday began on the evening of October 31st but was celebrated all through the day on November 1st until sunset. November 1st was the official start of the winter season, and this is the third pagan harvest festival on the Wheel of the Year.

Samhain is pronounced like *saw-win* or *sah-ween*, and the second pronunciation contributes to our modern word Halloween (All Hallows' Eve, shortened and corrupted with the *-ween* part of Samhain). On this day, the Celts marked the finality of the harvest season and prepared for winter, when the Cailleach would reign again over the land.

The Celts believed that if the Dagda and his wife, the Morrigan, chose to mate over the river where they met and first fell in love on Samhain, then the next harvest would be a bountiful one. Whether or not the gods coupled that year, Samhain was always a raucous and joyous occasion for the Celts, despite the fact that it was a winter-welcoming ceremony.

Many cultures, the Celts not excepted, associated winter with death—crops did not grow at this time, and game was scarce, either because of hibernation or migration. However, this did not stop them from celebrating Samhain. As pagans still believe today, the ancient Celts believed that the veil between the real world and the spirit world was the thinnest on the evening of Samhain (October 31st). They believed that not only could their dead ancestors visit them, wishing them luck and prosperity, but that unsavory ghosts could also trouble them.

This is where the tradition of wearing masks and costumes comes from. If a harmful spirit or entity cannot recognize the costume-wearer, how are they supposed to cause them harm? Later Celtic tradition saw people carving faces into turnips and leaving them to dry like shrunken heads, which was another method to ward off unwholesome spirits. These evolved into our jack-o'-lanterns of today (Irish immigrants used pumpkins in the New World instead of turnips).

Taking a look back at the ancient Celts, many burial mounds from the Stone and Bronze Ages keep time with this ancient celebration that is halfway between the autumnal equinox and the winter solstice. It is likely that the Celts, as they often did, built enormous bonfires around or on top of these burial mounds to welcome the spirits of the dead, as well as to honor the last of the light part of the year while welcoming the dark half of the year. The burial mounds were hugely significant at Samhain because of the belief that the spirits of the departed could come and go during this night.

It is probable that Samhain, like other major Celtic holidays, included sacrifices, mostly animal but possibly human. Records for this holiday were only set down in detail in the early modern age, so some of the practices we associate with the Neopagan Samhain and with Halloween do not have roots tracing all the way back to the Bronze and Iron Ages. It is almost certain the Celts marked this important occasion with fire, and it is almost just as certain that animals like bulls or goats would have been sacrificed and/or purified during this festival. Feasting and merrymaking definitely happened, as it was a time to celebrate, a kind of final hoorah before the land began to freeze.

Samhain and Beltane are at opposite ends of the year and were the most important holidays to the Celts. This is not so much because of crop harvests as it was due to the importance of raising livestock. The Celts had a system of pasturing their animals in summer and winter fields, and this clear delineation between the two halves of the year was mainly due to the need for shepherds and farmers to take care of their livestock. Crop planting and harvesting were essential to each and every holiday, but the reason these two festivals are so important (Samhain, the winter, and Beltane, the summer) was because of livestock, or so 19th-century scholar Sir George Frazer writes.

Chapter 6: Celtic Mythological Beasts and Entities

Each and every culture, modern and ancient, has its own creatures that make up legends, myths, and bedtime stories. Most of the following Celtic creatures and beings are still spoken of today with a hint of discomfort or even fear for those who are skittish. Others love spine-chilling stories of monsters and ghoulies, and whether you love these stories or they creep you out, they're still fascinating.

These creatures aren't all bad. Some are creepy, some are terrifying, and some are simply amusing. Which one is your favorite?

The Banshee

The banshee is likely the best-known mythological export from Ireland besides the leprechaun. She is often depicted as a grotesque hag with thin, long, flowing white hair, claw-like hands, and dressed in black. However, she can sometimes appear as a lady of indeterminate age in a white dress or as a young woman wearing a mourning veil.

Woodcut depiction of the banshee as a crone.
https://commons.wikimedia.org/wiki/File:Banshee.jpg

The most terrifying aspect of the banshee is not how she appears or what she is wearing. It is that she appears at all because the appearance of a banshee and the subsequent wailing she performs are said to predict death. If you see/hear a banshee, either you or someone close to you will die. This is why the banshee is likely the most feared of all Celtic mythical creatures. Her eyes are said to be red-rimmed and bloodshot from constantly crying, and that would admittedly be terrifying to behold in the gaunt face of a woman wearing tattered clothing in a foggy bog.

There is a theory on where the myth of the banshee comes from (although many people today swear that banshees are no myth and that they do wander the moors of Ireland). In ancient Celtic funeral rituals (as in many places in Asia), some women were paid to mourn an important person's death. Their wails became known as keening, and today, we use the word to describe a high-pitched scream or cry that eagles often make, as well as infants or adult humans.

The legend of the banshee is alive and well today in the countryside, although her status as a mythical creature is slowly being supplanted by rational explanations of hearing her keening. Some say the banshee's wail is the scream of a rabbit or a fox, and if you have ever heard either of those sounds, that is a spot-on explanation. Proponents of the existence of banshees ask, how then does one explain a death so close after hearing the "banshee's" wail? Coincidence?

Dearg Due

The Irish vampire comes in both male and female forms, but this particular story concerns the female version.

The story goes that there was once a young woman who was in love with a local boy, but her father did not take her feelings into consideration whatsoever. The father promised his daughter to a powerful chieftain, but this chieftain was not the man the woman loved. He and his family also had a reputation for being brutal and cruel.

The chieftain and the stunningly gorgeous young woman were married, and of course, there was a huge celebration, but the bride and her love were miserable. And family life with the chieftain provided no relief. He would lock his bride up for days or weeks at a time. She starved herself out of misery, and the chieftain remarried quickly, seemingly unconcerned. The father did not care either. The chieftain had provided him with a handsome bride price for the beautiful (now deceased) girl.

The dead girl's grave had only one bereft visitor—her love, the man she was not permitted to marry. According to legend, the spirit of the dead woman simply left the grave because her lust for vengeance and her anger were that strong. One can only hope that the man she loved did not see this terrifying sight.

The spirit of the woman, compelled by her thirst (pardon the pun) for revenge and by her blind rage, made her way to her childhood home and killed her father in his sleep.

Her next step, as you can imagine, was her evil husband's home. According to most stories, as she burst into his chambers, likely looking like a ghostly nightmare, he was in bed with several women, with no care at all for her suffering or her memory.

The woman-spirit disregarded the other people present in the bed, throwing herself onto her husband and killing him almost immediately. Then she proceeded to do what she did not do with her first kill—drink all the blood from the body.

After she drained him of his blood, she began to feel an unquenchable thirst for human blood. She then became known as the Dearg Due or Red Bloodsucker, and she spent her undead existence luring men with her ethereal beauty to dark places to kill them and suck out their life force. She is said to even dress in red, emphasizing her deepest desire.

With every kill, the doomed Dearg Due became more and more ravenous, the hunger and thirst for blood ever more powerful. She was known to be insatiable. One wonders if her lost love, who visited her grave every day, transferred some of his feelings of revenge and retribution to her spirit, feeding her own want of vengeance and prompting her to rise to seek her own form of justice.

The male version of the Irish vampire is similar to the traditional story of the undead monster in only a few respects. There is a relatively modern (so the ancient Celts would not have told this story) tale about an evil dwarf, Abhartach. He terrorized the town of Derry until a hero slew him. However, the hero buried him upright (as one would), and the next day, the dwarf came back even more evil and despotic than he was before. The hero slew him again, but the same happened.

A wise Druid told the hero to slay Abhartach again but to bury him upside down to keep him from rising from the dead once more. This tactic worked.

The vampire connection comes with the idea of rising from the dead, but it also has its place in another legend concerning the vicious, bloodthirsty dwarf. He drinks the blood of those in town, another vampiric trait. Instead of a Druid, a pious Christian tells the hero that in order to slay the "walking dead" blood-drinking dwarf, he must stab the dwarf with a sword made of yew and then bury him upside down. But he must also place a huge stone slab on the grave while surrounding it with thorns—one can only presume as an extra precaution.

One thing that sticks out in the Abhartach legend that parallels the typical vampire story is that the hero was told to kill the dwarf with a yew sword. Yew has been revered for millennia, especially by the Celts and their Druids, for its association with the power of death and its magical properties. Voldemort from the *Harry Potter* series possesses a wand made of yew wood.

The Dullahan

Although across time and many different countries and cultures, the concept of a headless horseman appears, we are, of course, focusing on the Celtic version, the Dullahan. The Dullahan is also not exclusively male, as this magical entity can take on a female form as well; however, it is most commonly portrayed as a male figure.

This imposing, frightening being either rides a black horse or is pulled along in a black carriage by six black horses. This carriage is known as the Black Coach or the Death Coach. It travels so quickly through the night that nearby branches and bushes will be set alight.

The Dullahan depicted with a headless horse.
https://commons.wikimedia.org/wiki/File:Croker(1834)Fairy_Legends_p0239-dullahan.jpg

As for appearance, the Dullahan dresses in all black and always carries its head with it. This head is said to have supernatural powers of sight, scoping out the land over long distances in search of the cursed people the Dullahan seeks to take the souls of. The head is said to have eyes that roam back and forth, left and right, constantly. The Dullahan can also hold its head high above its shoulders, using it as a periscope to search out its victims. Again, the Dullahan is most commonly depicted as a man, but there's really no strict gender reference.

If you come across the path of the Dullahan as he rides his hell-horse or is pulled along in the Black Coach but are not his intended victim, you still have a price to pay. He will likely spare your life, but he will blind you. His supernatural head will stare into your eyes to complete the deed. If you try to avert your eyes, the Dullahan will either pour a bucket of blood into your face to blind you or whip you across the eyes with his whip made from a human spine. Charming.

If you *are* the one the Dullahan seeks, there is no way you can lock this powerful being out. All doors, gates, windows, trap doors, and anywhere you can hide will fly open at his command, and all he has to do is say your name for your soul to flee from your body.

If this sounds terrifying to you, you are not the only one. The Celtic entity known as the Dullahan is sometimes said to be the embodiment of the Celtic god Crom Dubh, whose name means "the dark one." His followers are said to have employed the use of human sacrifice more than the average group of Druids, and Crom Dubh is said to have a constant battle over light and dark, as well as over the harvest, with the god of skills, Lugh. Crom Dubh, who is depicted as a dark, hooded figure, evolved into the concept and physical manifestation of the Dullahan.

If you carry pure gold with you, you may hold off the Dullahan for a time. If it is a golden necklace or even a gold coin, this may protect you the first time he sees you, but it isn't a talisman that has a permanent effect. Where the banshee's wail provides a warning or an augury of death to someone close to you, the Dullahan's appearance assures it.

Why is the Dullahan depicted as headless? The main theory, besides the fact that a headless being in all black carrying a supernatural, bright-eyed possessed head and a whip made of human spine cantering down the moors on a horse like a bat out of hell is absolutely bloodcurdling, the Celts, as we mentioned in previous chapters, held special beliefs about the human head. The Celts thought the soul resided in the head. That is why sword pommels were often carved into the shape of human heads (for power) and why the Celts are written to have kept the heads of their enemies in Greek and Roman sources. This practice wasn't so much to usurp their enemies' power like some cannibalistic tribes did and still do; it was more a talisman that served as a reminder of the power of their enemies, which they now possessed.

Balor

Known as Balor of the Evil Eye, he is the king of the Fomorians, the demonic race that was eventually defeated by the Tuatha Dé Danann before humans came to inhabit Ireland. We will discuss more about the Fomorians below.

Balor was the chief of the whole race, and he became Balor of the Evil Eye when he looked upon a powerful magic potion his father's Druids (yes, humans were not the only ones to have Druids) were brewing, and the fumes got into his eye. Typically, the tales depict Balor as a giant with only one eye, much like the Greek Cyclops. The difference between Balor and the Cyclops is that Balor's eye constantly shoots a stream of burning, destructive light and heat that destroys everything it falls upon each time he opens his eye.

Some stories say that Balor has two or three eyes, but they all agree that one of the eyes is the "evil" destructive one that he used to bolster the Fomorians in their fight against the god race, the Tuatha Dé Danann. In fact, unless he constantly wishes to burn everything in his path or close his only eye, this interpretation holds the most water. He can use his normal eye or eyes while covering the malignant eye with a leather shield, as is mentioned in one version of the story.

Balor is actually the grandfather of the god Lugh, whom we have mentioned several times. Lugh valiantly kills his own grandfather and beheads him. Another version of the story has Lugh shooting a sling stone through Balor's eye with a blow so powerful that the stone emerges from the other side of Balor's head. When the giant falls, he crushes twenty-seven of his fellow Fomorians.

Fomorians

This is the demonic race that Balor championed. Balor was actually a chieftain, not their king—the Fomorians were led by King Indech. Above, we mentioned that Balor's fallen body crushed more than two dozen of his comrades in arms, and we must remember that most Fomorians were not giants like he was.

Group of Fomorians off to battle.
https://commons.wikimedia.org/wiki/File:The_Fomorians,_Duncan_1912.jpg

They were known as the "demon race," which inhabited the Irish Isle before being defeated by the gods, who subsequently were driven underground by humans. Therefore, the cataclysmic battle between the Fomorians and the Tuatha Dé Danann took place before humans were said to have come to Ireland.

Describing the appearance of Fomorians is challenging because they did not take on one specific form. There didn't seem to be any uniformity of appearance, and since they were demons or demon-like, perhaps they could choose their appearance at will. Some are described as those who dwell in the underworld or in the depths of the sea, and in the 7th century, the Fomorians took on personas as raucous sea marauders, no doubt due to the Viking invasions of Britain and Ireland. But as for looks, some are completely cloaked; some are small, hairless, long-eared, and wear only loincloths; and some resemble half-baked forms of animals like horses or goats. They often are described as having only one arm or one leg or even one eye, so they were basically all malformed in some way.

However, it should be noted that some of the gods, such as Lugh, are products of deities mating Fomorians. The ones that the gods took as mates were, of course, beautiful. This begs the question raised earlier if the demon race could appear as they wished or if their appearances were something that could not be helped. Besides the more than occasional coupling and even marriages between the Tuatha and the Fomorians, the two races did coexist for ages until the final battle between the two occurred.

It is also said that the Fomorians could have been antagonists against the gods *and* the first humans in Ireland. That is what the Celtic legends say—that the first humans had contact with both the gods and the Fomorians and that they could have seen this epic battle between the races.

Pooka

Changing pace from hell demons, soul-stealing, and battles of epic celestial consequences, we now introduce the Pooka. The Pooka (or *Púca*, in the Irish spelling) is a shapeshifting creature that can bring either good luck or bad luck to households, depending on the treatment it receives.

The Pooka reminds one of the brownies, which are more popular in Scotland and are said to help out with household chores while a family sleeps as long as it is left a bowl of milk at night. The Pooka has several recorded appearances, but it is normally described as brown, small, hairy, and may or may not have a tail. The Pooka usually wears a dark cloak, whether in humanoid or animal form. Even when in humanoid form, the Pooka will have a tail—perhaps that is why it always has a cloak handy.

The Pooka has a proclivity for mischievous behavior more than anything particularly harmful. If it chooses to take the form of a pony or a horse, for example, it can lure a rider onto its back and run as fast as it can through terrifyingly uneven terrain, frightening the rider out of their wits and then dropping them off in the middle of nowhere, technically unharmed, while the Pooka laughs and gallops away. If one were ever to suspect an encounter with this type of Pooka, it is said that it can be controlled if the rider is wearing a pair of sharp spurs. This will disappoint the Pooka but will save the rider from the prankster's plans.

The other side of the Pooka is auspicious and even selfless. One story has it that a Pooka appeared to a young farmer as a bull, and the farmer took the bull in and gave it food and a warm cloak. In return, the Pooka, as a bull, did mill work, plowing, and other heavy labor. In Pooka form, it would clean and organize the barn at night. One night, the boy saw the Pooka in his true form, but unlike most mythical Irish beings, Pookas willingly introduce and show themselves to the humans they interact with. The two became friends and exchanged gifts over their friendship.

Some stories also tell of Pookas, who can see other magical entities otherwise invisible to humans since they are magical themselves, throwing themselves in the way of beings wishing to cause harm to unsuspecting humans, thus saving the humans. The Pooka will then reveal themselves to the human, and the grateful human will likely strike up a friendship with the creature that saved them.

Aos Sí

The Aos Sí is, in simplest terms, the name for the magical race of faeries and otherworldly beings that inhabit Ireland. In fact, the name Aos Sí or Sídhe is synonymous with faerie. This isn't what we typically think of as "fairies," the tiny insect-like humanoid beings that adorn themselves with flowers and live in tiny houses in the woods. Although those beings are part of the faerie race in Ireland, Aos Sí is an umbrella term that includes all magical beings, whether they choose to reveal themselves to humans or not, hence the spelling we use here, faerie.

Depiction of Aos Si riders in 1911.
https://commons.wikimedia.org/wiki/File:Riders_of_th_Sidhe_(big).jpg

Even the dreadful Dullahan is said to belong to this race of faeries or Fey in Ireland. The origin of the name Aos Sí is typically traced back to a phrase meaning "people of the mounds" or "people of the fairy mounds." This goes back to the gods going underground after being defeated by the Milesians, the legends discussed in Chapter 4 in Ériu's section.

Celtic tribes were very careful not to offend the people of the mounds. Burial mounds were considered sacred places where festivals could be held, some specifically built to light up during certain solstices and equinoxes, but before and after festivals, during ordinary days, these places were treated with respect and caution.

Many legends in Ireland state that if a human becomes entranced by any being of the Aos Sí or if they eat any of their food, the human will become trapped in their world and not be able to return to the world above ground. They will never be seen again by any of their kind.

As for not offending the faerie race, they are often not referred to directly by name—euphemisms like the Fair Folk, the Folk, or the Good Neighbors, along with Sídhe or Aos Sí, are used even today. The Celts would set out offerings of milk, fruit, or sometimes bread to appease these beings.

Some sources say that the Aos Sí were the remnants of the Tuatha Dé Danann, the race of the gods, after the humans pushed them underground. The Aos Sí live in a liminal space between the two worlds, which is why humans can see them if they reveal themselves and can interact with humans if they choose. Banshees, Pookas, or leprechauns would be included in this designation.

Sluagh

One of the more intimidating creatures on our list is the Sluagh, or the "host of the dead." These fearsome faeries-gone-bad are said to fly in the air in a crescent formation, much like birds, and swoop down to take the souls of those they prey upon.

Before Samhain and Imbolc and the other major fire festivals of the ancient Celts, some origin stories of the Sluagh say the Celts were forbidden from lighting fires on these occasions because the space between worlds was so thin. The Druids warned that fire would attract the Sluagh. However, at some point, that practice was abandoned in favor of huge bonfires and offerings to the dead and other spirits.

The unforgiven souls, the Sluagh.
https://commons.wikimedia.org/w/index.php?curid=93481

The Sluagh typically travel in large groups, hence their name, and they are said to be the souls of unforgiven dead people. We've already mentioned two versions of the Sluagh—the ancient Celts thought they were part of the Aos Sí, the Fey Folk who had been corrupted in some way, seeking to make humans as miserable and lost as they had become. After Christianity was introduced to Ireland, the belief in the Sluagh persisted, but the lens from which they were viewed changed. They were seen as unforgiven sinners bent on dragging happy, thriving souls down to hell with them when they swept down over the earth.

Although there are so many more mythical beings to cover, we will end on a whimsical note rather than a creepy one. We hope this chapter has encouraged you to check out Irish folklore for yourself to explore the enchanting and often terrifying world of the Fey.

Glas Gaibhnenn

Glas Gaibhnenn is the cow of plenty and fertility. Said to be owned by a smith, this cow is light green in color or has green spots, making it easy to pick out. This cow never runs out of milk, so for a culture dependent on the favor of good weather for its harvests and to feed its domesticated livestock, Glas Gaibhnenn was a symbol of plenty and of comfort because of its consistent ability to provide.

Balor in disguise stealing the enchanted cow.
No restrictions;
https://commons.wikimedia.org/wiki/File:Myths_and_legends;_the_Celtic_race_(1910)_(14596782139).jpg

One interesting legend Glas Gaibhnenn is involved in is one in which Balor of the Evil Eye steals the cow and takes it to a glass tower. This tower also holds his daughter, whom he never lets leave because it is prophesized that she will give birth to a son who kills Balor (Lugh, as mentioned before). The hero Cian must take back the cow from Balor of the Evil Eye, and he ends up becoming the father of Lugh. Lugh is conceived, and the cow is returned to its rightful owner. All is well until the major battle between the Fomorians and the Tuatha Dé Danann.

Chapter 7: Celtic Legends and Stories

In this chapter, we will be covering some essential Celtic tales that sometimes get overlooked in today's retellings of famous Celtic legends. The famous stories that every Irish person is somewhat familiar with will be covered in Chapter 8.

The Sons of Tuireann

Sometimes, this tale is known as the "Tragedy of the Sons of Tuireann." Tuireann does not feature in this story other than his part as the father of three sons: Brian, Iuchar, and Iucharba. Tuireann has another three sons, but this is not their story. The previous three sons' mother is Danu.

As for Brian, Iuchar, and Iucharba, their mother is Tuireann's own daughter, Danand. During the great battle, the Mag Tuired, in which the Fomorians are overcome by the Tuatha Dé Danann, the same battle in which Lugh kills Balor of the Evil Eye, Tuireann's sons, Brian, Iuchar, and Iucharba, actually kill Lugh's father.

In short, Lugh kills Balor, his own grandfather. Tuireann's sons kill Cian, Balor's son and the father of Lugh. This is where the "Tragedy of the Sons of Tuireann" begins, a tale that is heavily influenced by Greek mythology and takes place in far-flung foreign empires.

Because they have killed his father, the god Lugh exacts a blood price, known in Irish as *eric*, and he requires the brothers to accomplish incredible feats and retrieve various magical items. Retrieving those magical items requires massive strength, cleverness, and fortitude. The items Lugh demands for the blood price include the following:

- Three golden apples from the Greek garden that the Hesperides cultivate. The Hesperides were akin to forest nymphs, and the brothers had to get past them, as well as the giant serpent guarding this mystical garden.
- A magical pigskin from King Tuis in Greece. This pigskin had the power to turn water into wine and cure disease.
- A poisoned spear from the king of Persia.
- Two horses from the king of Sicily, Dobar, who were able to pull chariots across water and land.
- Seven pigs that were the property of the King of the Golden Pillars that, if eaten at night, would reappear in the morning.
- The mythical dog Failinis as a puppy, which was known as Lugh's companion (after the brothers get the puppy from the king of Iruaith).
- The cooking spit that belonged to the women of Inis Fionnchuire, which was located much closer to home than the first few items. The significance of this cooking spit is that these women were of the faerie race, and they lived underwater. The brothers also return to Ireland with the previous items before setting out again to retrieve the cooking spit. The faerie women laugh because they could easily overpower any of them and let the brother who dives down to retrieve the spit take it because of his audacity.

There is one final task. Unlike the other tasks, which required feats of cunning and strength to capture or acquire items, the final requirement is something the three brothers must do.

This last task takes place atop the Irish hill of Miodhchaoin, or it is meant to. The three brothers must shout at the top of this specific hill to complete the *eric* and be free from Lugh's obligatory enchantment. However, this hill is occupied by the sons of Miodhchaoin, and he and his three sons stab Brian, Iuchar, and Iucharba with spears.

The sons of Tuireann manage to kill Miodhchaoin and his three sons (their trials made them formidable warriors), but the three sons of Tuireann are all mortally wounded. Brian lifts his brothers' heads, and the three of them complete the task as best they can, using the last air in their lungs to weakly cry out so that the final task is fulfilled.

Iuchar and Iucharba die soon after, and although Brian still lives, he barely has any life left in him. He does have enough to entreat Lugh to use the enchanted pigskin they retrieved to heal his brothers (and one can presume himself), but despite all that they have done to fulfill the *eric*, Lugh refuses to use the pigskin to heal any of them. Tuireann buries his sons, dying himself soon after, one can say perhaps of a broken heart.

The ultimate winner of this story is the god Lugh, whom some may say cruelly denied mercy to the men who killed his father. He profited immensely through the acquisition of these magical objects, with the spear becoming his famed weapon and Failinis his faithful canine companion. In a way, the "Sons of Tuireann" is as much about Brian, Iuchar, and Iucharba as it is an origin story of sorts for Lugh, who is celebrated during the Lughnasadh festival.

The Faerie Folk

Where does the story of the faeries come from? They are ubiquitous throughout Celtic and Irish stories, and many people still believe that their existence is possible in forested areas far away from human civilization.

The short answer is that the Fey Folk or the faeries, which can appear as beastly creatures, evil apparitions, deities, or beautiful, magical beings, originate with the godly race of the Tuatha Dé Danann. The race of the gods was the predecessor of sorts of the Fey Folk, and the faeries remained behind in the spaces between this world and the other.

The origin story of the Tuatha Dé Danann, the race of the goddess Danu, the ever-living ones, may have seemed clear-cut from our other stories about them, but things began to get cloudy when Christianity arrived in Ireland and histories began to be written down.

Before this, oral tradition was the only way that lore survived besides artistic depictions. The Druids famously never wrote any of their knowledge down because they were so protective over it. It was only in the 9th, 10th, and 11th centuries that visitors to Ireland began describing the Tuatha Dé Danann as deities from the clouds rather than simply shapeshifting, mischievous or benevolent beings. This idea was an attempt to say that the Christian God was greater than any other gods, and it changed Celtic pagan practice to honor the Tuatha Dé Danann through the lens of godhood rather than simply beings to be honored and feared.

The bottom line is that the boundary between the race of the gods and the race of faeries is very blurred, and they have similar abilities. Faerie folk essentially remained at the edges of the human world while the gods went underground to be revered without being directly viewed.

The Origin of the Harp

The harp has been an enduring symbol of Irishness for as long as anyone can remember. The Dagda's enchanted harp has the power to change the seasons. Ireland has had the harp on various currencies for centuries, and today, Irish euro coins still bear the harp on the obverse side.

The origin story of the harp begins with Cana Cludhmor, who is sometimes referred to as Canola, a corruption of her Irish moniker. Cana Cludhmor is said to be the Celtic goddess of inspiration, dreams, and, of course, music, likely due to this story. One evening, she had a fight with her husband, and Cana Cludhmor chose to take a walk along the beach to calm herself down. She ends up reclining and falling asleep, and she hears delightful music in her dreams.

When she awakes in the morning on the beach, she realizes that the music she was hearing was not only in her dreams; it was being created by the wind, which was gently and steadily blowing through the sinew stretched across the ribcage of a rotting whale carcass. The tale is charming up to that representation. But the ultimate takeaway is that Cana Cludhmor becomes inspired to create the harp based on this example made by chance in nature. It's a good thing she and her husband had that disagreement!

Chapter 8: Famous Stories: The Children of Lir, Cú Chulainn, and Tír na nÓg

These are some of the most beloved and well-known stories in Ireland today, and they all stem from Celtic tradition and mythology. These stories have enchanted and amazed legions of people from all generations stemming back centuries, and they've been the inspiration for countless modern pop culture references and world-building. Why did these stories, particularly these three, stand the test of time to the point that there are even several variations of each? We will answer this below, and we will also stick with the most traditional and widely accepted version of each.

The Children of Lir

The Children of Lir, also sometimes referenced as "The Fate of the Children of Lir," is a tragedy told over and over and even studied in Irish schools.

After the death of the great Dagda, there was a need for a new ruler of the Tuatha Dé Danann. Lir wanted to be elected king, but he was passed over for Bodb Dearg, who was elected the new ruler of the Tuatha Dé Danann. Lir was understandably upset, as he had missed out on the role, but in order to get Lir's loyalty and appease him, Bodb offered Lir his daughter Aoibh's hand in marriage. Lir accepted, and he pledged his fealty to Bodb as the new ruler.

Lir and Aoibh's marriage was a happy one, and they had four children together. These children were the light of their lives, but after the birth of the set of twins, Aoibh died, and Lir was distraught, as were the children. Bodb Dearg was heartbroken, but he did send another one of his daughters, Aoife, to Lir to wed.

Because both her father and her new husband doted on her four stepchildren, Aoife became jealous. It only took about a year for her to cultivate feelings of unworthiness and anger against them. She even pretended to be sick during this year of mental anguish and perceived slights, thinking that she had lost Lir's love because of his obvious love for his children. Aoife even went as far as to plan to kill them outright. She got her entourage together and promised them riches beyond compare if they would slay the four children. Her entourage, of course, refused, so Aoife, in her hurt and rage, took up a sword herself. But she could not go through with the bloody deed.

It was then that she forced the children into a lake to bathe, and once they were in the water, she transformed them into swans. However, these were no ordinary swans—they kept their personalities, intellect, reason, and speech. They also had the ability to sing songs of incomparable beauty.

Aoife set a time limit (albeit a ridiculously long one) on their curse, with some versions saying at the eldest child's request. The four children were to remain as swans for three hundred years in the lake in which they were transformed, then spend three hundred years in the cold north of Ireland, and then a final three hundred years as swans on a lonely, desolate island.

Instead of returning to the castle of her husband, Aoife returned to her father's castle. Bodb asked her why the children weren't with her, and she made up a story about how Lir did not trust Bodb with his own grandchildren. Bodb did not believe this nonsense for an instant, and he sent a message to Lir, saying that his four precious children were missing.

When Lir received this message, he searched for his children, eventually coming to the lake where they were bound to remain for the next three hundred years. Four gorgeous white swans came to him and revealed themselves to be his lovely children. Lir wept at what Aoife had done. The eldest informed him that they were to be cursed like this for the next nine hundred years. To ease his pain and lull him into a restful sleep, the children sang their lovely swan songs to their beloved father, and he fell into a deep, dreamless sleep.

Lir discovering his children, now swans.
https://commons.wikimedia.org/wiki/File:Ler_swans_Millar.jpg

When he awoke, Lir headed to his father-in-law's castle and informed him of what his daughter Aoife had done to the children. Bodb's anger and grief filled the castle, and he immediately said that Aoife's suffering and torment would be even greater than the children's could ever be. Bodb asked his daughter what the worst being was that she could imagine turning into, and she answered that it was a demon of the air. So, she became one forever. Bodb turned Aoife into a demon of the air, and she is cursed so to this day.

During the first three hundred years of the children's curse, people, gods, and Milesians alike came to hear their heart-stirring and unbelievably beautiful music. However, the time eventually came for them to move north to the cold rivers and lakes at the Maoilé, where they had to spend the next three hundred years singing. It was at this time that killing swans became outlawed throughout Ireland. Their time at the Maoilé was trying and full of suffering. A severe storm once separated the siblings, and although they were eventually reunited, the end of the second three hundred years could not come soon enough. They were all ready to get out of the north.

Finally, when the time came, the children flew to Iorrus Domhnann in the northwest of Ireland to complete their last three hundred years as swans. Here's where certain versions of the story differ. Some versions say that it was so cold in Iorrus that one night, the waters froze, and the poor swans' feet stuck fast to the ice. They then prayed to the one true God and professed their faith in him, which freed them from the ice. Other parts of the story leave this out, and the swans are simply said to endure their time in the northwest for the next three hundred years. What is normally told in all the versions of the Children of Lir is that during their time in Iorrus Domhnann, there was a young man they met who recorded an account of their story.

When their full nine hundred years of being cursed were over, they flew back, still in swan form, to the home of their father, Lir.

When they reached their homeland, the children were distraught to find that the lands of Lir were abandoned, appearing as if there hadn't been any inhabitants for long enough that everything appeared overgrown and lay in ruins. Dismayed, they traveled to the island of Inis Gluairé, where many birds congregated. They could at least live in peace with other birds and with each other.

After St. Patrick Christianized much of Ireland, there were still many who remembered the children of Lir, including a holy man ringing a bell for prayers. When the children heard the bell, they were frightened, but the eldest said that perhaps they should listen to the bell calling out the time for prayer, as it could break the curse. When they had all finished listening to the bell, they sang an otherworldly, enchanting song. When the holy man came to the shore of the lake to hear their song, he asked them if they were indeed the Children of Lir, for he had heard of their ancient plight and was actually in the area to track them down.

The four swan children put their trust in the monk, allowing him to put silver chains on them and lead them away from the lake. The king of Connacht's wife heard of these swans being the tragically cursed famed children of Lir, and she demanded that the monk bring them to her at once. The monk refused, and so the king went to take the swan children by force. As soon as he touched them, the curse was broken—all their feathers fell off to reveal four extremely aged and bony people, three men and a woman, the nine hundred years taking their toll instantly. Apparently, this disturbed the king of Connacht so much that he left immediately.

The legends line up here to say that the children knew they were close to death and asked the monk to baptize them. He did as they requested, and he buried them soon after.

So, what does this story teach us, and why is it so popular even to this day? The Celtic symbolism in the story and the connection to the mystical and magical Tuatha Dé Danann is one reason. Another reason this story is so popular in post-Christian Ireland is that it shows that accepting God brings peace and freedom. This is, after all, one interpretation. There is even a statue of the four children in their swan form in Dublin. The Fate of the Children of Lir is just a part of Irish cultural heritage as the harp, Irish Gaelic, and the rolling green hills.

The statue of the Children of Lir in Dublin.
https://commons.wikimedia.org/wiki/File:Children_of_Lir.jpg

The Great Cú Chulainn

Every Irish person knows the story of Cú Chulainn, the great warrior who was half mortal and half immortal. Cú Chulainn is likened to Hercules, Ireland's version of Achilles, and other great warriors from other mythologies, but the similarities end when their birth origins and enormous strength are discussed.

Even from a very young age (some sources say seven years old), Cú Chulainn possessed massive strength, which he achieved by essentially turning himself inside out. This was frightening enough to those who would harm him, but his rage gave him enough strength to singlehandedly hold back armies. The mental image this evokes is quite disturbing, but it is how the legends talk about his unbelievable strength and power.

Cú Chulainn was not always the name of this young, powerful legendary figure in Irish mythology. He was born to a mortal mother who named him Sétanta. He was given the name Cú Chulainn, literally meaning "Hound of Chulainn," when he was a young boy. Chulainn was a blacksmith with a fearsome guard dog, and the child Sétanta killed the dog while defending himself, to everyone's shock. Chulainn was understandably distraught that this superhuman child had killed his dog, but Sétanta offered himself up as Chulainn's security guard until he could find and train another guard dog for the man. Whether or not he succeeded in finding Chulainn another hound is up for debate since the stories differ, but Sétanta was forever known as the Hound of Chulainn.

Sétanta kills Chulainn's hound.
https://commons.wikimedia.org/wiki/File:Cuslayshound.jpg

There are multitudes of stories and legends involving this son of a mortal woman and Lugh, the god who is master of all skills. Cú Chulainn's prowess in battle and his good looks (when he wasn't raging out) make sense when one realizes he was the son of the great Lugh.

As a young child, Cú Chulainn was trained in martial arts by Scáthach, the warrior woman of Scottish legend. She gave him his spear and taught him to fight, although when he went into his rage fits, he really had no control and would trash anyone and anything in his way. During the time of Cú Chulainn's training, it was prophesized that he would be enormously famous but that he would have an early death, much to the dismay of those who loved him.

One of the most famous stories involving him is when Queen Maeve from Connacht attempted to take over the territories of Ulster. Cú Chulainn is with a woman in the forest when that happens. As the Ulster troops struggle to hold off Queen Maeve's forces, Cú Chulainn joins the fray pretty much when the last Ulster man falls. He goes into rage mode and singlehandedly beats hundreds of men in Queen Maeve's army, becoming the hero of Ulster.

As prophesized, Cú Chulainn died young, with most sources saying at the age of twenty-seven (he was seventeen when he defeated Queen Maeve of Connacht). Maeve conspired with several noblemen to draw out the Hound of Chulainn so that they could slay him. In Celtic culture, there were grave taboos that must never be broken. If they were, the person who broke them would become not only weak physically but also spiritually and emotionally. The two taboos that Cú Chulainn were faced with were eating dog meat or refusing hospitality. One day, he comes across an old crone who offers him dog meat that she is roasting on a spit. Trapped between these two taboos, he accepts a sliver of dog meat and eats it.

Thus, Cú Chulainn has broken one of the most severe taboos of his culture, and he is in a weakened state for the upcoming attack. Lugaid, one of Maeve's conspirators, has three magical spears made, each designed to kill a king. The first spear is used to kill Cú Chulainn's chariot driver, the king of drivers. The second spear is used to kill Cú Chulainn's horse, the king of horses. And we all know for whom the third spear is intended.

After Lugaid mortally wounds Cú Chulainn with the third spear, Cú Chulainn pulls all the strength he has left to tie himself to a tall stone so that he can die facing his enemies on his feet rather than on his knees. A beam of light is said to have shone on Cú Chulainn, and when his sword arm drops, it cuts Lugaid's hand off. A raven then lands on the hero's shoulder, signaling that his breath has left his body.

The stories of Cú Chulainn could fill many more pages; this is simply an introduction to the famed Irish hero, whose only weakness was that he broke Irish taboos, which could happen to anyone. Nowadays, the Hound of Chulainn is a symbol of Irish nationalism and identity. He is not so much a mascot as a legendary figure that the Irish take pride in, and the town of Dundalk's motto is "I gave birth to brave Cú Chulainn." This is because the stone that Cú Chulainn tied himself to so he could die with dignity is said to be in Dundalk.

Cú Chulainn's image has been placed on Irish coins and military medals, made into bronze statues, and depicted on flags and other Irish nationalist materials. There is no way the Irish people will forget about Cú Chulainn, his bravery, or his many exploits any time soon.

Tír na nÓg, the Land of the Young

This tale is truly one of the most provocative, beautiful, and heartbreaking tales that have been handed down through the centuries on the isle of Éire. When listeners hear the story of Tír na nÓg, it is almost impossible not to be moved in some way. This is why stories about this enchanting land free of aging and pain are told today.

We will focus our story of Tír na nÓg on a princess from the Land of the Young, the beautiful Niamh (pronounced niav) of the Golden Hair. This is the story of how Niamh from Tír na nÓg and Oisín of Ireland met and fell in love. There is one variation to the story, which we will get to at the end, so make sure to pay attention to the first telling and then see how the alternate story changes things.

Oisín, his father Finn MacCool, who is a hallowed Irish hero in his own right, much like Cú Chulainn, and the Fianna, the hunter-warriors with whom they travel, behold a gorgeous maiden on one of their many adventures. She has long flowing hair, full lips, and bright, shining eyes. None of the men have ever seen any living being so beautiful in all their years.

The maiden introduces herself as Niamh to the band, and she looks upon Oisín (pronounced a bit like "ocean"), informing him that she has heard tales of the Fianna and the famed young Oisín MacCool and that she had left her land specifically to find and marry him.

All present are a bit confused and stunned, especially when Niamh tells them that she comes from Tír na nÓg. They all know the meaning of the place's name—the Land of the Young, of the Unageing, the Land of Eternal Youth. They never consider that Tír na nÓg is an actual place, so naturally, they react with disbelief. Niamh continues to describe her homeland with such detail that the band cannot help but conclude that there must be some truth to what she is saying.

Niamh explains that her land is the most beautiful place imaginable and unimaginable. There is no death, no sickness, no pain, and no aging. Whatever one's age is when one arrives in Tír na nÓg becomes their eternal age. Niamh says they must not tarry long, though, as the effects of leaving Tír na nÓg will begin to affect her, although much more slowly than any mortal who comes to the Land of Youth and then leaves.

She professes her love to Oisín (whom she has just met, so this may seem odd to us, but it is a story, and she is extremely beautiful). Niamh begs him to come away to her home, where they will both stay young forever and live to their hearts' content, with all the jewels and gold they could ever imagine and all the delicious feasts they could ever consume. Oisín is almost convinced, but he agrees to go on one condition: that he is eventually permitted to return to Ireland to visit his beloved father. Niamh, of course, agrees to this sensible request, and father and son have a tearful, heartfelt goodbye. The Fianna are sobered by the loss of their second-in-command.

Oisín and Niamh traveling to Tír na nÓg.
https://commons.wikimedia.org/wiki/File:15_They_rode_up_to_a_stately_palace.jpg

So off Oisín and Niamh travel on her silver horse, over and through oceans, viewing spectacles unseen and hearing songs unheard by any mortal for centuries except for Oisín. He is amazed at the fantastic plants and animals he has never seen. He sees a gorgeous grove of trees laden with shining fruits and says to Niamh, "Is this your home?"

She then laughs and replies, "This place cannot even hold a single candle to my homeland. You will know when we reach Tír na nÓg."

On and on the horse canters, through valleys and mountain ranges of gold, through more verdant forests, even through the sky and seas, and eventually, they reach Tír na nÓg. Oisín realizes Niamh was right. He has never felt happier, lighter, or more relaxed than he does when they cross into Niamh's native land. Not even his greatest battle victories can compare to the elation he feels in Tír na nÓg.

Oisín and Niamh quickly marry and have many children together, and the couple never ages. They only grow to love each other more and more as they live, never getting sick and never knowing any strife or unhappiness. Their children grow and prosper but stay forever youthful. Everyone has as much to eat as they need and more. The plants and animals are sources of endless joy for the family and the other inhabitants of Tír na nÓg.

One day, as if awakening from a dream, Oisín remembers the promise that he made to his father to come back to Ireland and visit. For the first time since he entered the Land of the Young, he is troubled. For several days, his brow is furrowed, and he wonders what he should do or even how he could reach Ireland. Niamh notices something is off with her husband.

"My dear love," she addresses him after a few days of observing him like this, "unhappiness is unheard of here in Tír na nÓg. However, I can see distress playing on your features. What could be troubling you so?"

"Niamh, my darling," responds Oisín, "these years with you here have been the happiest I could have ever asked for. It's just I've remembered the promise I made to my father, Finn MacCool, and to the Fianna. I miss my father terribly, and I wish to visit Ireland to fulfill my promise."

Niamh provides her love with a horse that can make the journey, but she cautions, "Dear husband, on your journey, you must stay in the saddle. If your feet touch the ground of Ireland, you may never ever return to me, to Tír na nÓg. Please return to me, dear Oisín. That's all I ask of you."

Oisín kisses his dear Niamh and promises to return to their home in Tír na nÓg right after he has seen his dear father in Ireland. So, he rides off on the faithful horse, and in what seems like no time at all, he returns to Ireland, the vibrant green hills dotted with buildings he does not recognize. These turn out to be monasteries and churches spread across the countryside. He sees a passing old man, and he hails him.

"Ho, kind traveler! What have you heard about Finn MacCool and the Fianna? I am his son Oisín, come back to embrace my father."

The old man looks up at Oisín on the horse first with surprise, then amazement, then a bit of sorrow. "I'm so sorry," the old man answers, "but Finn MacCool has been dead these past three hundred years. The Fianna are tales of legends and fireside stories now, but we remember their glorious deeds."

Overcome with sorrow that his father has passed, Oisín unsurprisingly wobbles in the saddle, but he soon composes himself, remembering Niamh's warning. *Truly, three hundred years have passed in my beloved homeland? It only felt like a few...*

Some stories go on to say that Oisín sees a group of men attempting to lift a beam out of the mud and stick it vertically on some construction project in the vicinity. Seeking a distraction and knowing he can solve their problem instantly, he rides over and leans to the side, heaving the beam up alone with ease. Suddenly, the girth of the saddle snaps, and Oisín and the saddle both fall off the horse and onto the ground. Three hundred years catch up with Oisín instantly, and he dies soon afterward, unable to return to his love in Tír na nÓg.

Before we discuss the significance of this enduring story, let's look at some alternative details that crop up in some versions. Sometimes, storytellers insert a mini-story alongside Oisín and Niamh's first journey together to Tír na nÓg. He sees a stunningly beautiful marble castle after they've passed through a sparkling sea, and he says, "Niamh! That is beautiful! Is that where you live?"

She answers, "No, this is not yet Tír na nÓg, but a horrendous ogre of a man lives there and keeps a princess as his prisoner. He is forbidden to wed her until he defeats another in battle, but no one dares to fight him, so they remain unmarried, and she remains a prisoner in that marble castle."

Her story moves Oisín, and he asks that they stop because he wishes to challenge the ogre to battle. Niamh readily agrees; after all, his bravery and strength were so legendary that she heard about him all the way in the Land of Youth. Oisín defeats the ogre jailer, and the princess is now free to do as she pleases. This makes Niamh fall in love with the young MacCool even more.

Another important variant has to do more with Tír na nÓg and the way that some stories say they select their ruler. Every seven years, there is a contest to determine the king. All contestants must run up a certain hill, and the winner becomes king. The current king has won for many years, although doubts are starting to creep in that make him worry about how many more times he can win the competition. He consults a Druid about the future of his rulership of Tír na nÓg, and the Druid assures him that he will remain ruler of the Land of Youth unless his son-in-law competes.

The king is relieved by this news since his daughter is still unmarried. He orders the Druid to turn his daughter's head into that of a pig. However, the Druid also tells the daughter, Niamh, that if she marries a son of Finn MacCool, her curse will be broken, and she will be herself again. This is why Niamh sets out to find Finn MacCool and the Fianna, and she chooses Oisín to be her husband. She tells them all about the curse and everything that happened and about her origins, and then they are wed. Then the journey of Niamh and Oisín back to Tír na nÓg begins. Once they return, the competition for kingship is held. Oisín obviously wins, and no one dares to run against him again.

Why does the story of Tír na nÓg persist today? There is even a scene in the movie *Titanic* where an Irish mother tries to lull her frightened children to sleep with stories of Tír na nÓg, a place where there is no fear, pain, suffering, and death, as the ship is sinking. Knowing the story of the Land of Youth makes the scene all the more poignant, as the children desperately cling to the words their mother tells them, all while she knows the truth.

A land without any sort of disease, suffering, and aging sounds appealing to a people who were subjected to rulers of various sorts for centuries, especially after English colonization. Tír na nÓg becomes a dreamland, an escape, and something inherently Irish to hold onto. However, many arguments have been made that a person cannot truly appreciate life in a place devoid of suffering. How can one recognize victory, justice, or joy if they have never experienced failure, despotism, or negativity?

Chapter 9: Origins of the Irish Language

The origins of languages starting back to when humans began to speak are almost impossible to detangle, although many scholars, linguists, historians, and scientists throughout the ages have attempted. It would seem that the most widely accepted theory is that there was a first language from which all others stemmed. There is a story in the Bible about how languages were created, which is likely where this idea came from initially (the Tower of Babel in Genesis, Chapter 11). However, after centuries of tracing languages, their families, resemblances to other languages, and how people have migrated across the globe through the ages, the (at least working) theory is that the "first language" did exist and is referred to as Proto-Indo-European.

With that being said, we wish to point out how complicated tracing linguistic roots can be. With changes in lifestyle, practices, ceremonies, clan relationships, and location, people change, and so does their language. The language spoken by the Celts prior to the Early Middle Ages would be entirely unrecognizable to Irish Gaelic speakers today.

We call this language Goidelic. If you recall in our earlier chapters, the Celts used to inhabit the Iberian Peninsula, parts of eastern Europe, and perhaps all the way down to Turkey. The language these far-flung Gallic and Celtic peoples spoke can be referred to as Proto-Celtic—the grandmother of the Goidelic language.

Proto-Celtic split into three "children" of sorts: Celtiberian, Insular Celtic, and Gallic. These three languages became distinctive because Celtiberian was used by those who remained in Spain, Portugal, and what is now the Basque area between Spain and France. Those Celts we know and love who sailed the seas and ended up changing Ireland forever are the originators of Insular Celtic. Finally, the third child, Gallic, was the Celtic-rooted language spoken by the tribes inhabiting modern France and Austria that gave the Romans a good fight before being conquered along with the Germanic "barbarians."

Insular Celtic is the language child we wish to focus on because the Goidelic that Celts in Ireland used developed out of this language, as well as another sibling that we call Brythonic. This is what was used in Britain, and it later evolved into the Cornish, Welsh, and Breton that are still spoken and written today. Goidelic evolved into modern Irish Gaelic (Gaeilge), Scottish Gaelic (Gàidhlig), and Manx.

We are concerned with Goidelic and its development. Its writing system, *ogham*, which we've touched upon, is normally considered to have been first used in the 3rd and 4th centuries. Scant examples remain because *ogham* was likely mostly written upon organic materials like wood that have not survived. The examples that do survive show us that Goidelic and Brythonic differed in which sounds were present. For example, Goidelic has the "qu" sound, which seems to have changed to a "p" sound in modern Gaelic, whereas the Brythonic languages did not seem to have the "qu" sound but did possess the "p" sound.

Popular Gaelic Words & Phrases

- *Uisce beatha*: This is where we get the word whiskey from! It means "water of life," and its roots are from two Proto-Celtic words preceding Goidelic. *Uisce* comes from *udenskyos*, meaning "water," and *biwotos*, meaning "life." We can assume the Goidelic versions of these words were some in-between versions.

- *Dia duit*: This simple phrase means "hello." This is a modern greeting, especially when compared to how the ancient Celts would have greeted each other. Most of that is a mystery, but it is likely they would have met with a strong handshake with a forearm grip just to make sure the other party wasn't stashing a weapon. *Dia duit* is modern Gaelic for "hello," but it means

"God be with you." They're not talking about the Dagda.

- *Sláinte!*: Cheers! This literally translates to "health," as many toasts around the world do.
- *Céad míle fáilte*: This charming phrase is found all over Ireland even today, and we can imagine a version of it existed in Goidelic because of the immense importance the ancient Celts placed on hospitality. It means "one hundred thousand welcomes."
- *Go raibh maith agat*: The Irish version of "thank you" literally means may you go with goodness. This is especially poignant when one thinks of the situation in which you would use this phrase, mostly upon saying goodbye, which is *slán*, meaning "safe." The Bronze and Iron Ages were not easy times to live in, but as we can see, the Celts did more than survive—they thrived.
- *Is fearr Gaeilge briste, na Bearla cliste*: This is a saying with a powerful meaning. It translates to "Broken Irish is better than clever English." This is a favorite phrase of proud freedom-loving Irish who resent English domination. It is just tongue-in-cheek enough to make its statement without being overbearing.
- *Gaeltacht*: This is a word that refers to a place or region that mainly speaks Irish Gaelic. It is often notated on maps or guides, and one can often see blatant Celtic influence in the area when it comes to historical sites and museums.

Why did we include modern Irish Gaelic words in our list instead of those the Celts would have spoken? Well, it's almost impossible to track down the Goidelic language in its spoken form, at least for concepts and ideas that would be familiar to us. Instead, Celtic thoughts and ideas remain with us through the artifacts they left behind, their burial mounds and monuments, and, most importantly, their descendants. Even though all Celtic languages are considered endangered by **UNESCO** today, they have undergone revival movements throughout the 18th, 19th, and 20th centuries by various groups attempting to preserve Irish and Celtic culture. Many of these groups do this for political reasons, and many simply understand that with the loss of a language comes the loss of rich history and cultural heritage.

Ogham, Again

Ogham (pronounced owam) was written from right to left, contrary to modern Celtic. It had twenty regularly used letters, but later on, an extra five letters were added on, but it is unclear when the use of these letters began. *Ogham* has all the sounds of English because the letter "q" did not have its own solitary symbol—it was written as the sound "qu."

Although when you compare *ogham* and Norse runes side by side, similarities seem to pop up at first, but upon closer inspection, it would seem that the similarities end when the realization hits that in order to carve symbols into hard surfaces, they, of course, have to be straight, rigid shapes. Some scholars still see a resemblance and thus a relationship between the two writing systems, and this is understandable since the two cultures definitely interacted with one another, with Vikings landing on Irish shores and eventually founding Dublin.

However, another theory, perhaps one that makes more sense since the presence of similar letter counts lines up, is that *ogham* is simply the Celtic way of representing the Latin alphabet. This might be more plausible since Celts, as far back as the Hallstatt and Gallic cultures, would have known the Roman Empire intimately. The Greeks and Romans visited and wrote about the Celts in Ireland, as we've established, and there may have been an exchange of language and ideas, that is if the eastern visitors deigned to speak with those whom they wrote about as barbarians.

Many Irish people and those with Irish heritage outside of Ireland (think the US and Canada) have begun to reclaim their ancient Celtic roots and craft *ogham* pieces or wear jewelry with *ogham* writing on it. They also create or purchase art pieces, jewelry, clothing, or other items with ancient Celtic motifs, which we will describe in detail in the next chapter.

Chapter 10: Celtic Art

Spirals and swirling depictions of humans and animals, intricate, knotted designs, golden brooches, and expertly designed torcs (collars) meant to fasten cloaks and denote wealth and status—these are just a few of the ways ancient Celts used art to express themselves in their daily lives.

During the Bronze Age, smiths produced untold amounts of bronze alloyed from copper reserves in Ireland and tin in Cornwall, England. Bronze was then created and expertly transformed into items that were not only useful but also beautiful. These included items like drinking vessels, horse tack, weapons, and farming implements, and they were exported all throughout Europe during the Bronze Age.

This was also when the Celts in Ireland produced a veritable fortune of gold products because of the gold deposits throughout the Emerald Isle. These golden objects have been found in abundance throughout Ireland, Britain, and continental Europe, meaning these objects were prized and sought after because of their quality, craftsmanship, and assigned value.

Tara Brooch

One of the best-surviving pieces of Celtic workmanship is the Tara Brooch. It is made from cast silver, and archaeologists date the brooch to be from around the 8th century. It is decorated in the La Tène style of art, which we will discuss in greater detail below. This art style influenced artisans from the time of the Hallstatt civilization all the way through to the Christianization of Ireland.

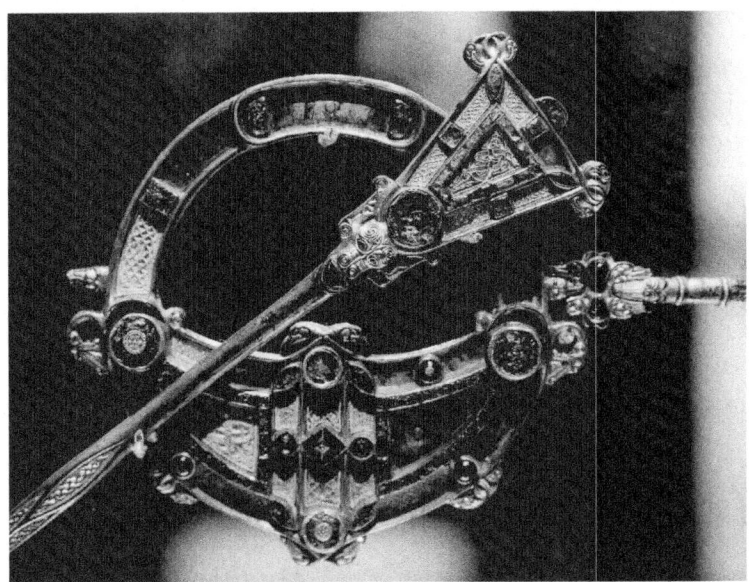

The Tara Brooch.
Sailko, CC BY 3.0 <https://creativecommons.org/licenses/by/3.0>, via Wikimedia Commons; https://commons.wikimedia.org/wiki/File:Spillone_di_tara,_da_bettystown,_contea_di_meath,_viii_secolo_02.jpg

The Tara Brooch gets its name from the legendary seat of the High Kings of Ireland, the Hill of Tara. This seems a fitting name for a piece that is so quintessentially Irish Celtic. The brooch has nothing to do with Tara or any legendary kings—it was simply called that by a salesman thinking to aggrandize his ware, which he purchased from a farmer woman in the mid-1800s who found it in one of her fields. The brooch is in a recognizable shape even to modern eyes because it has a round outer side and a pin that goes through that circle, like an ancient safety pin.

This is also the shape and size that Roman brooches were made, and they were not as delicate as the Tara Brooch, which leads historians to conclude that the Tara Brooch had a purely ornamental function rather than actually binding cloaks to the wearer. It would not be strong enough for a brooch's traditional purpose.

Muiredach's High Cross

This massive, towering stone cross found at the Boice Monastery (Monasterboice) is part of a group of three similar crosses, but this particular piece is known to be the most exquisite.

Muiredach's cross is over five meters tall (more than fifteen feet), and it is made of sandstone, which is easier for artisans to carve than other types of stone. Sandstone is also plentiful in Ireland. Although this cross is not the tallest of the three (the West Cross is seven meters tall), it is the most intricate and detailed.

This standing cross is full of Christian iconography, but interestingly, it is all done in the traditional Celtic art style, covered with knots and twisting vines. It even includes the sun and the moon, which are represented by two soldiers. These may be references to the ocean and to the earth goddess Gaia. Celtic art, especially the art exemplified in this cross, retains its characteristics and style no matter the subject matter. This cross was commissioned to show various scenes from the Bible, such as the crucifixion of Christ, possibly Christ's seizure and arrest by Roman soldiers, and Christ giving the key of heaven to Peter.

The western face of Muiredach's cross.
Adriao, CC BY-SA 4.0 <https://creativecommons.org/licenses/by-sa/4.0>, via Wikimedia Commons; https://commons.wikimedia.org/wiki/File:Mainistir_Bhuithe_cross_Muiredach.jpg

Charmingly, there are other symbols throughout the cross. For instance, the bottom of the cross on each side features two cats, animals long associated with magic. There is a ridiculous amount of ornamentation, including men's heads surrounded by winding snakes, centaurs, wrestlers, and abundant horsemen, along with about a dozen other biblical scenes.

Muiredach's High Cross is an essential part of Celtic history because it shows how Celtic culture and Christianity blended in Ireland, and it preserves the artistic style used about 1,200 years ago for viewers and scholars today.

Battersea Shield

This stunning piece dates from the Iron Age and also emanates the La Tène style of art that was prominent in most Celtic art pieces during the Iron Age, Bronze Age, and after. Even though it is only part of a shield, its purpose is obvious.

The Battersea Shield piece that survives today is the bronze outer plating for a shield that would ordinarily have a wooden backing and perhaps some sort of strapping or padding for the user. These materials have long since degraded, but the bronze plate is stunning.

Battersea Shield.
British Museum, CC0, via Wikimedia Commons;
https://commons.wikimedia.org/wiki/File:British_Museum_Battersea_Shield.jpg. Image has been flipped

The Battersea Shield, now located in the British Museum, is an important example of ancient Celtic craftsmanship because there are four structural bronze pieces and three decorative bronze pieces all fused together seemingly by magic. The smith was able to hide where they attached the pieces into its overall design, so the pieces are held together seamlessly. This gorgeous shield is decorated with red glass ornamental studs. The museum insists that the shield was made in Britain, but the La Tène style and Celtic design contradict this.

What Made Celtic Shields So Important?

Shield-making in the Iron and Bronze Ages contributed new techniques that made shields more useful in actually protecting the wielder from attacks. Celtic broadswords were huge and fearsome, and the shields had to be made to withstand these attacks.

In Celtic culture, weapons, armor, and shields seemed to take on personalities and attributes of their own, and Celtic warriors often thought of their weapons and gear as partners in battle rather than mindless implements. There was a famed shield called Ochain, which is said to have screamed whenever its owner was in danger. Its scream caused all other shields in Ulster to shriek out along with it.

The predominant shield design in the ancient Mediterranean and hence most of Europe was rounded. But the Celts preferred to make their shields tall and flat, like rectangles, with a protruding bump bulging out from the center. This was simply for the benefit of the user because it added more room for their arm, thus giving the person greater maneuverability. Of course, it took time to get the design right; nails holding the shield together would often pierce the wearer's arm on impact, so the design needed tweaking.

There were shields specifically made for battle, and these may have a central adornment where the protrusion was but little else in the way of ornamentation. And then there were shields like the Battersea Shield specifically made for ornamental and/or ceremonial purposes. For those of high status, like royalty and chieftains, decorative shields were often made to be buried with them. Archaeologists have uncovered many shields from the Celts in great condition because they had a habit of sacrificing them to the gods by tossing them into rivers and lakes, which has kept them in excellent condition.

Let's Talk About La Tène

After the rather utilitarian and geometric Hallstatt and Urnfield styles came the La Tène style, which is named after the site, La Tène village in Switzerland, where thousands of artifacts in this distinctive style were found.

What makes this style unique and prevailing throughout Celtic civilizations both on the islands and the European continent is the maturity of stylistic thought during the creation process and the idea of beauty and functionality. So much of this artistic style survives because around the time when La Tène was developing, between 480 and 190 BCE, these ancient civilizations switched from cremation to burial as the preferred method of interring the dead. This is why so many of these artifacts survived.

La Tène art is responsible for the gorgeous golden torcs, the intricate brooches, and the carefully carved and decorated weapons and everyday objects (plates, drinkware, knives, hair accessories, etc.) the Celts were famous for. This period is when Celtic design and expression flourished.

This period is where we see the familiar S-scrolls intertwined, the curving foliage patterns, and other knotted motifs, which survive until even today. This is similar to Norse patterns on shields and their own art and metalworking. Some animals included in these famous Celtic designs were wolves, owls, snakes, and ferocious wild boars. The Celts even included human forms and sometimes figures from their pantheon and mythological stories on their chariots and weapons.

It is important to note that the La Tène style, which is intrinsically insular Celtic (despite the prevailing thought by historians that the "stylistic maturity" of the age is from contact with the Greeks and Romans), is found in textiles, metalwork, and even surviving stone and wood carvings. However, there are almost no paintings, sculptures, or pottery examples of this style. This is interesting because it shows us which objects the Celts placed particular reverence on and respect for—which items to show off and which to create simply for utility's sake.

Chapter 11: Celtic Rituals

It may surprise you to learn that some normal, everyday activities people in Ireland and even around the world do today have some root or origin in rituals practiced two thousand years ago.

One main tradition that carries over is storytelling. When the Celtic civilization arose, spread, and then flourished, everything was still passed down orally. Even the Druidic rites and knowledge were never written down—all Druids and their acolytes had to memorize the entire canon of Druidic knowledge. The Druids were so secretive that modern Neopagan Druids can only guess what their ancient predecessors truly believed and practiced.

No, storytelling, a pastime still very much alive in Ireland and one the Irish are quite adept at, stems from the Celts having a rich tradition of passing down their tales and their real histories through oral tradition. It wasn't until monks came to Ireland that these tales and histories began to be recorded.

One reason storytelling and ancient histories have survived is because the bards, the story keepers, worked alongside the monks, as long as they were permitted to, in order to keep Celtic culture alive, at least in story form if not practice. With the arrival of St. Patrick, the bards' and Druids' offerings to demons were banned, as was animal sacrifice.

The Importance of Fire

The Celts believed fire to be cleansing, which is why giant bonfires were lit at nearly all of their annual festivals. Fire represents light, the sun, warmth, and fertility. Celtic societies cremated their dead until the 5th century BCE, as did many other ancient peoples—many around the world still do.

Fire is said to keep evil spirits away, and it's easy to make this jump. There were many dangers to Bronze Age peoples, not the least of which were wild animals and other people who may wish them harm. Fire helped provide a sense of community and security, as the fireside is often where storytelling took place. Humans have always had a close relationship with fire, and even today, sitting around a fire and looking into the flames, we can remember our ancestors who did the same.

Animals were often sacrificed to the Celtic pantheon on bonfires during festival days, although this was later outlawed by the Christian monks and St. Patrick.

Life Cycle Events in Celtic Society

Nature

In general, the Celts held natural places of great beauty to be sacred, like forest groves, trickling streams, or mighty waterfalls or rivers. These sites were often unmarked for ritual use, but they were just as often marked with little shrines and sites where offerings were given.

At these shrines, the Druids would take offerings from the communities they served, such as grains, jewelry, fresh meat, honey, choice fruits, and other valuable goods, and give them to the gods they served in these sacred places of nature. If a good like a weapon, shield, piece of pottery, or artwork was offered, it was often broken before being offered to the gods.

The tradition of leaving milk out for Pookas or Fey Folk, which is practiced even today by some superstitious people, may have had its origins in ritual offerings to the Celtic gods of old.

Many people still burn sage as a cleansing agent after a bad experience or to make sure an area is safe from harmful spirits. This was a practice the Druids often employed. The combination of sage's powerful smell and the cleansing properties of fire joined to sanctify places and people. In order to cleanse a person, the ashes of the burnt sage were smudged onto them, usually on their forehead.

Holidays

In Chapter 5, we mentioned the main festivals Celts would have celebrated throughout the year. Many of these are still celebrated today, although under the guise of Christian celebrations (St. Brigid's Day on Imbolc/February 1st and Christmas/Yule). Halloween and All Saints' Day on November 1st is the most notable change; originally, this was the Samhain celebration. However, Wiccans and Neopagans around the world still celebrate Samhain without human or animal sacrifices.

Children

Celtic beliefs concerning children line up with the thoughts the whole Western world had about them up until the Industrial Revolution. Children weren't considered fully formed humans until they could speak, which would be between two and three years old. However, if a child died, there was quite a juxtaposition between how they were perceived while they were alive and how they were buried. Children's graves from Celtic burial sites were positively festooned with jewels and valuable objects. In death, it seems families overcompensated for the way they thought of their children in life.

Weddings

Incense is lit to purify the air, and ritual handwashing is performed at several stages throughout the ceremony. These rituals are still performed at Celtic weddings today. Three candles, which represent unity, are lit by the spouses. One candle represents the families of each of the spouses, and the third and final candle they light represents the creation of a new family.

There is also a tradition that comes from Scotland but is Celtic in origin, and that is the Stone of the Jury. The couple holds a stone where they are holding the wedding ceremony, which is always outdoors. The stone represents the ancestors and the earth, and as the couple makes promises to each other, they hold the stone together. This is also a way to ask the ancestors and nature to bless their union. After the wedding vows, this stone is then plopped into a river. Sometimes, the couple keeps the stone after the ceremony.

One meaningful ritual often present in a Celtic wedding is the prayer of protection. A circle is drawn around the couple to protect them in their own separate dimension, as the Druids did with standing stones and circular shrines. These circles can be made with stones, flowers, or pieces of wood.

Marriage and Divorce

Men and women were shockingly equal in Celtic society two thousand years ago. It is unclear whether women could become Druids or bards, but they could hold other positions of authority and had the freedom to marry whom they chose under Celtic tribal law. This is not how things always played out, but men and women had similar, if not the same, rights under the law. The Druids were the keepers of the law, and if a particular chieftain gained the loyalty of a certain corrupt Druid, he could bend the law to his own desires.

There were actually *nine* types of marriages that could take place in Celtic Ireland.

1) The man and the woman each take equal financial responsibility during their union.
2) The man contributes more financially.
3) The woman contributes more financially.

In these three, which were the most common, no dowry was required, but a bride did take her valuables with her, and they stayed in her possession. In case of divorce, she had her own possessions and would not be dependent on other parties. When we say financial contribution, we mean possessions coming into the marriage since working within marriage was typically farming and regular household chores. These three marriage arrangements were a precursor to the modern prenuptial agreement.

4) A man simply moves in with a woman.
5) The couple elopes without getting the bride's family's permission.
6) Involuntary abduction, meaning no consent from the families.
7) "Secret rendezvous," which can be interpreted to mean that the couple meets without either of their families' knowledge and eventually either elopes or makes their relationship public.
8) Marriage by rape.
9) Marriage of two insane people. This one is up for interpretation.

Polygyny, or having two or more wives, was permitted, but women could not have more than one husband, at least under the law. However, both parties were not required to be monogamous.

Circumstances in which a woman could divorce her husband include if he seduced her or lied to her in order to get her to agree to marry him, if he is impotent or too obese to have sex with, if he leaves her to have sex with men exclusively, if he beats her to the point of leaving visible marks, if he fails to provide for her, and if he leaves her for another woman. A woman could even divorce her husband if she found out he was telling tales about their sex life.

Grounds for a husband divorcing his wife included if she mistreated him physically and/or verbally, if she ran off with another man, or if she was sterile. But women asking for divorce was much more common, if divorce was common at all.

Death

In most cases, it is unclear how the deceased were dressed prior to burial, but we do know from extensive archaeological evidence that feasts were held near the gravesites to honor the deceased, and we know they were buried with pottery filled with foodstuffs. If the dead was a warrior, they were buried with their armor, weapon, and shield. If the deceased was a weaver, they would be buried with the tools of their profession—spindle, loom, perhaps even spinning wheel, needles, and other textile-making materials.

The dead were buried with their jewelry and valuables unless some were set aside as heirlooms to be passed down. Objects that were buried with the dead were often ritually broken before being interred, just like the offerings to the gods we mentioned earlier.

PART THREE:
Patterns of Change (430– 600 CE)

Chapter 12: Here Comes St. Patrick, 432 CE

Palladius

Patrick is credited with bringing Catholicism to Ireland, which has heavily shaped its national identity. However, there is reason to suspect, based on papal correspondence and records that exist from the 430s, that St. Patrick was not the first Catholic missionary to the Emerald Isle.

That title belongs to Palladius, a freshly ordained bishop whose family was from Gaul. He was sent by the pope to the believers who already existed in Ireland at the time. Since St. Patrick is regarded to have landed in Ireland in 432, Palladius's journey is estimated to have taken place just a year before.

One thing to note is that there were two purposes for which missionaries were sent to far-flung locales. One was to bring Christianity to people who had never heard of Jesus and where there was no established church or monastery. The other purpose was to bolster the believers who were already there and to make sure they were following the orthodoxy laid down by the Roman Catholic Church (remember, that was the only branch of Christianity that existed at the time). From time to time, sects would pop up that had different (unorthodox) ideas from what was professed by the church.

At the time Palladius was ordained, the pope wished for him to check on the people of Britain and make sure that if they were engaged in some sort of heresy that he put them back on the orthodox track, so to speak. The main threat at the time was Pelagianism, which emphasized the human nature of Christ and suggested that the divine and human aspects of Jesus loosely existed together in one entity. Pelagius also attested humans were born good, so babies were born without sin (rather than the prevailing idea of original sin). Pelagius believed that Christians could essentially achieve their own salvation. Once they accepted Jesus as Christ, then that would preclude them from even wanting to sin, and they would simply live a righteous, ascetic life. Pelagius was branded as a heretic, and bishops were dispatched to the European continent and Asia Minor to ensure his followers stopped their errant beliefs.

Palladius was sent on a mission to the believers in Britain and Ireland. It is unclear whether he was meant to visit the Scots or the Celts, but he likely went to Ireland first. This is because when he arrived in Wicklow, he was soon banished by the king of Leinster. He then went to visit the Scots in Britain. Therefore, he is pretty much forgotten as the first bishop to Ireland, and this is for several reasons.

One reason that Palladius and his mission are overlooked is that historically, the record blurred the lines between him and Patrick. Since Patrick likely landed back in Ireland as a bishop (we will tell his story shortly—this was not the first time he went to Ireland) the year after Palladius's failed mission, records do conflate the two, including the dates of their death.

However, we have enough evidence to conclude that Palladius did make his mission to Ireland, was there very briefly, and then went back to where he felt most comfortable. Most reports that we have now say that he and his companions were banished almost as soon as they arrived in Wicklow. Some accounts say that Palladius was then killed, but this is not the majority opinion. Most historians now and then stick with the story that Palladius went to the Scots in Britain and to monasteries and congregations that had already been established. And now St. Patrick enters the story.

Saint Patrick, the Patron Saint of Ireland

If you are unfamiliar with the story of St. Patrick, this should be a fascinating look at a famous missionary. We do not know the name that Patrick was born with; he most likely took the name Padraig (Irish) after his ordination and return to Ireland. Sources from half a millennium later suggest several names he may have been called as a youngster, but there is no way to know for sure.

Stained glass portrayal of St. Patrick.
Nheyob, CC BY-SA 4.0 <https://creativecommons.org/licenses/by-sa/4.0>, via Wikimedia Commons; https://commons.wikimedia.org/wiki/File:Saint_Patrick_Catholic_Church_(Junction_City,_Ohio)_-_stained_glass,_Saint_Patrick_-_detail.jpg

In fact, the date of his arrival is also shady. We mentioned that St. Patrick returned to Irish shores in 432. However, this date may have been chosen to maximize the veneration of Patrick and minimize any information about Palladius's mission, which happened the year before. This is because the earliest dating of Patrick's landing was from a century after it supposedly happened. This is an example of writing history backward because you favor a certain person over another.

Patrick was not actually Irish. He grew up as a Roman citizen in Britain, but he was stolen by Irish pirates when he was young. He worked as a shepherd in Ireland for about six years. In his famous *Confessio*, Patrick writes that he was not yet a Christian at the time of his abduction, despite the fact that his father was a deacon and his grandfather a priest. However, time in captivity amongst his sheep provided him with ample opportunity for reflection and prayer, and it was during his time as a slave that the young Patrick embraced Christianity.

After six years as a shepherd, Patrick writes that he heard a voice telling him to flee to a ship, that he was going home. Patrick then traveled more than two hundred miles to a port, and he eventually convinced the captain of one of the ships to let him board.

Once the captain was finally convinced to let this scruffy escaped slave join the voyage, they sailed for three days and landed in Britain. The crew wandered around through the country for about a month. The story goes that they were weary, hungry, grouchy, and bedraggled when Patrick prayed for sustenance for the crew. They then came upon several wild boar, and the captain began to see Patrick in a new light.

Eventually, Patrick made it back to his family, and he became ordained as a bishop. He wrote that he had a vision of a saint bringing him a letter from the people of Ireland, welcoming him back and saying they had a great need for him. Strangely, Patrick also landed in Wicklow, just like Palladius, and just like Palladius, he was chased out. However, unlike his predecessor, which he likely knew nothing of, Patrick simply traveled farther north until he found a place where he was welcome.

Now, why was Patrick so successful in changing the face of Ireland forever, planting and sowing the seeds of Catholicism that still grow today? Many say it was because Patrick had lived and worked among the Irish, and although he was taken as a slave by an Irish master, he held no ill will toward them at all. He loved the Irish people, and unlike many missionaries before him in other places, he respected their pagan practices. Because he reached out with love and a bit of compromise, his mission was a resounding success.

Patrick was able to explain difficult concepts, like the Trinity (Father, Son, and Holy Spirit), to the Celts by using the three-leaf shamrock that grew all over Ireland. It is one plant, but it has three essential parts that come together to form it. He also had a hand in merging Celtic holidays, such as Imbolc and Samhain, with Christian festivals and feast days. St. Patrick is one reason we have such beautiful standing crosses and other pieces that meld Celtic artistry and Christian iconography because they were allowed to coexist to a degree. Patrick condemned animal and especially human sacrifice, but he often used the Celts' existing ideologies to explain concepts about the Christian God, such as the Celts' veneration for nature (God created it).

This doesn't mean that Patrick's time amongst the Irish was easy. In fact, it resembled his time as a slave. Because he refused to accept gifts from prominent members of society, he offended them and, in turn, had no one to protect him. He was beaten and robbed plenty of times, even spending two months as a slave again at one point.

Yes, Patrick did use the shamrock to spread the notion of the Holy Trinity across Ireland. Yes, he changed some of the Celtic practices that were repugnant to the church and melded Christian celebrations with other practices. No, he did not banish the snakes from Ireland. Ireland has never had snakes, so this story is just one of the many fanciful apocryphal stories that are associated with someone whose life history does not have that many contemporaneous sources. We do have Patrick's own writings, the *Confessio* and the *Epistola*, the latter being a letter to the soldiers of a man who was excommunicated for enslaving some of Patrick's converts. But they are short and lack detail.

Patrick mostly won over the Irish people because he concentrated his efforts on prominent figures in society. Once kings were converted, their subjects usually followed. He also converted many wealthy women to Christianity. If these women's families objected to their choice, the women would simply leave with their money and join nunneries, sponsoring their nunnery and the construction of others. There was a huge wave of monasteries and nunneries built in the century after Patrick's death, and this can be traced back to him and his followers. He preached in Ireland tirelessly for forty years, becoming the most venerated saint in Irish history. His feast day, March 17th, is fairly calm even in Ireland—its raucous bender-like celebration overseas would likely give St. Patrick quite the shock.

Chapter 13: Paganism versus Christianity

We hope that the previous chapters about the Celts and their culture and practices have given you some type of an outline of their beliefs, which in modern times we simply refer to as paganism. Each culture around the world has ancestors that practiced (and some still do practice) forms of paganism or animism, which are religions that are specific to that region or country and usually involve nature and/or ancestor worship. For our purposes, we are referring to Celtic paganism in this chapter.

Side by Side

Paganism	Christianity
Many gods, some more powerful than others, different personalities, some vengeful and some benign, all to be revered.	One God, manifested on Earth in the form of Jesus of Nazareth. The Holy Spirit is the third part of the triune God, explained later.
Gods appeased and pleased with offerings, festivals, and sacrifices. The gods and goddesses are also revered and pleased with retelling their flattering exploits and legends.	God simply wishes that everyone love one another. Jesus was the sacrifice who rose again after three days. When he left Earth for heaven, he gave his followers the Holy Spirit, God's

Paganism	Christianity
	representative on Earth.
Festivals include Samhain, Yule, Imbolc, Ostara, Beltane, Litha, Lughnasadh, and Mabon. These are all seasonally based on the changes of the year and equinoxes/solstices. The Wheel of the Year essentially revolves around nature and the harvest.	Major festivals include saints' feast days, which may or may not replace pagan celebrations; Christmas, which was placed during Yule to celebrate Jesus' birth; and Easter, taking the place of Ostara in the spring.
Nature is holy, especially when it comes to sacred groves, majestic waterfalls, stunning mountaintops, or flowing rivers and deep lakes.	Holy places are sites where saints performed miracles; monasteries and churches are where believers gather to pray.
No central authority; each household can observe certain practices differently. However, if there is a serious issue, the Druids may be called upon to settle it.	Congregations made up of families from the same village listen to their priest; larger areas have bishops. These are representatives of the pope, and they are his mouthpieces.
The Druids hold all the wisdom and knowledge associated with the veneration of nature, divination, interpreting the will of the gods, and advising civil leaders. There is no written canon—everything is passed down orally for secrecy.	Local monks are the reason we have so much information about Celtic paganism. They wrote down *everything*, and the 5th century is when we began to see an explosion of writing and illuminated manuscripts in Ireland.
The dead were cremated at first, but this practice eventually fell away as people buried their dead in burial mounds with many personal items.	Community cemeteries in villages held the dead grouped together.
Nature is the absolute final authority. The waters, forests, and mountains are all to be looked at	God is to be revered for creating nature; nature is never to be worshiped for its own sake.

Paganism	Christianity
with awe and adoration. Fire is purifying and essential.	
Spells, amulets, special charms, and daily practices like candle lighting and paying tribute in the form of votive offerings play huge parts in the daily practice of the veneration of the gods.	There is only one God, and he is venerated through prayer. In the 5th century, it was still uncommon for people other than the clergy and monks to be able to read, but listening to the Bible was another way to venerate God.
Witchcraft (the practices mentioned above) were part and parcel of daily life, especially during important festivals like Samhain and Lughnasadh.	Witchcraft was forbidden. St. Patrick was so successful in his missionary endeavors because he used pagan practices to explain Christian ideas and practices. He patterned much of his converts' thoughts using what they were already familiar with.
Ultimate values: strength, reverence for nature, attuned to the seasons, virtuous, hospitable, fierce in battle	Ultimate values: one God to be worshiped, love one's neighbor as oneself, spread the message of Jesus Christ

Both paganism and Christianity have frameworks for life after death, although they are different. It is obvious that the Celts believed in the afterlife because even before they began burying their dead rather than cremating them, the deceased were buried with all that they would need for their next life. Unlike the concept of Valhalla for the Norse, it's difficult to peg down what Celts thought the afterworld would be like. Evidently, they thought it would be much the same as this world since their dead were sent away with edibles, potables, weapons, weaving materials, and sometimes even pets.

Christianity's concept of death and the afterlife was still quite new at this time; it was only four centuries after Jesus of Nazareth's death, and although the religion was making headway in Europe and Asia Minor, Christianity still had a long way to go. Christians of the time did think that believers in Christ would join him in heaven, and it was common for them to get buried in cemeteries that housed both pagans and Christians in villages or towns. Being buried on monastic grounds was reserved for clerics and those who held powerful community positions.

There is a story of St. Patrick in which he prays to God to help him make the pagans of Ireland believe in God, and God gives him a vision of purgatory. God says to Patrick that showing this vision to the people will convince them. It was meant to be a powerful picture of how awful the fires of hell were and the glories and joy of heaven. The Catholic concept of purgatory, heaven, and hell was well formed by this point, informed by various popes and church leaders.

One thing that was ingenious or enraging, depending on your perspective, was that Christian leaders like St. Patrick used existing holidays the Celts already celebrated and appropriated them as holidays in the Christian calendar. This is a phenomenon employed by many clerics and missionaries throughout the Western world when converting pagans to Christianity. It was very successfully done in Ireland. However, even to this day, Christians celebrate the Christian version of the holiday, and modern-day pagans (Neopagans) do their best to recreate pagan holidays in a way they find respectful and authentic of their ancestors' practices.

Both Irish Catholicism and Celtic paganism represent national identities that are sometimes at odds with each other but sometimes work together for common goals. For example, the monks worked closely with the Druids to record common daily practices of the Celts for posterity's sake, as well as other knowledge the Druids felt like sharing with them. These were learned men speaking respectfully with each other. Although violence and anger did erupt between the old and the new, Catholicism and paganism in Ireland had lived fairly peacefully for at least a century. Catholics fought much more heartily and viciously with Protestants than they ever did with pagans.

After all, paganism is a peaceful belief, only seldom invoking the gods for warfare and using human sacrifice. Christianity definitely has a much bloodier history, with its leaders eschewing the teachings followed by the early church (loving, helping, and healing) and following whatever paths they wanted. The Crusades are an excellent example, as are pogroms against Jews and infighting between Catholics and Protestants. Paganism was never responsible for levels of violence like those historical tragedies.

Chapter 14: The Decline of the Celts and Paganism

The Rise of Christianity

The 5th and 6th centuries in Ireland saw the rise of Catholicism and the decline of Celtic paganism. Despite the fact that St. Patrick and other clergymen on the island ingeniously appropriated pagan holidays and rebranded them as Christian ones, used Celtic iconography to explain their new message, and worked closely with the Druids to write down recent history, paganism still fell into the fringes while Catholicism took over.

In many countries and regions around the world, Catholicism exists beside native pagan practices like animism and ancestor worship, and there was a certain flavor of that in Ireland as well. Laypeople (people not part of the church leadership) often blended practices they had grown up with and the new ideas they had accepted about there being one God in the form of the Holy Trinity. Technically, Christianity itself expressly forbids this and demands devotion to Jesus only; however, policing villagers in far-flung rural areas has always been a challenge.

Even though the Irish Celts were able to keep some of their ancient practices alive, most of Ireland turned to Catholicism over the next three centuries after St. Patrick's ministry. Ireland became known and is still nicknamed the "Land of Saints and Scholars" for the virtual explosion of monasteries and churches founded in the 5th and 6th centuries and onward.

Why was this flourishing of monasteries and nunneries so successful in 5th-century Ireland? This question must first be answered by looking at St. Patrick's main mission model, which was to travel to each of the many smaller kingships that made up the whole of Ireland and preach his message to the king there. This was four decades of work, as Ireland had many of these little kingships, but if Patrick was successful in converting the king, the nobility and the commoners would eventually follow. Of course, St. Patrick spent plenty of time with rural villagers, but his main plan of action was to start with those in power and work downward.

Because Ireland was split into so many kingships and pockets of different authority, the decentralized nature of monasteries and nunneries fit right into this culture of independence and self-reliance. Indeed, most of these institutions had their own farms, animals, weavers, smiths, horses, and anything else they might need. The monks spent their days illuminating manuscripts, collecting Celtic oral tradition, and putting that information down on paper. There was much less attachment in monastic life to the whims or authority of the pope, which suited the Irish just fine. That does not mean that the clergy or monks went against the pope—they were simply used to governing themselves, and the model that the many kingships had already set out was adapted quickly and easily for the Christianization of Ireland.

Illuminated page of the Book of Matthew.
https://en.wikipedia.org/wiki/File:LindisfarneFol27rIncipitMatt.jpg

Appropriation of Holidays

Samhain is easily the most recognizable of the pagan holidays that the Catholic Church adopted and changed to fit its agenda. Even today, when we learn about Halloween, we know that it is a tradition that came with Irish immigrants to the United States during the Great Potato Famine. What is sometimes also discussed is Halloween's pagan roots, which date much further back than the 19th century.

October 31st began to be known as All Hallows' Eve and was eventually shortened to Halloween. In Christian Ireland, practices began to evolve that were at once familiar (dressing in costume, making protective charms, eating special treats, etc.) and new. Some of the new explanations for the holiday is that instead of dressing in special costumes and masks so as not to anger dark spirits, people would wear this protection to ward off Satan himself. The concept of a devil was foreign to the Celts, but the concept of malevolent spiritual beings was not. Each Samhain, every household would make a charm to protect them from these beings and hang them over their doors. It resembles St. Brigid's cross, which was no doubt adapted from these charms, not the other way around.

St. Brigid's cross, probably appropriated from the goddess Brigid.
Culnacreann, CC BY 3.0 <https://creativecommons.org/licenses/by/3.0>, via Wikimedia Commons; https://commons.wikimedia.org/wiki/File:Saint_Brigid%27s_cross.jpg

Jack-o'-lanterns, as they eventually became known, were either used as lanterns for those who walked from house to house, or they were set on stoops or porches to ward off evil spirits. These practices were recorded as early as five hundred years ago, and combined, we can recognize the modern practices of trick-or-treating and carving pumpkins. There were some differences, though. Trick-or-treating probably originated from the aforementioned practice of disguising oneself, in which folks would put on costumes and go from home to home asking for food (sometimes soul cakes, a special Samhain treat), fuel for the bonfires, or even offerings to the Fey Folk for the holiday. This was accompanied by the practice of carving monstrous faces into turnips and either using them to light the way as they went or as protective totems outside the home. The modern reader can easily see the traditions leading to our practice of Halloween festivities today.

Plaster cast of turnip jack-o'-lantern.
Rannpháirtí anaithnid at English Wikipedia, CC BY-SA 3.0
<*https://creativecommons.org/licenses/by-sa/3.0*>, *via Wikimedia Commons;*
https://commons.wikimedia.org/wiki/File:Traditional_Irish_halloween_Jack-o%27-lantern.jpg

Keep in mind that all of those activities were still practiced long after Ireland was Christianized. Those practices evolved and changed, but most of the Samhain practices stayed around in some form until church authorities forbade them relatively recently, like in the 18th and 19th centuries. These include making wine offerings to the sea and using stones for divination around the bonfires to see who around the fire would live another year. Some Irish never forgot these practices and simply kept doing them, mixing Samhain traditions with their Christian religion.

All Saints' Day eventually "replaced" Samhain, as the day after October 31st was the official celebration of the halfway point between the autumnal equinox and the winter solstice. November 1st was appropriated by the church as a day to venerate the saints, but many of those rituals and practices to do so, such as lighting candles, mimic the lighting of bonfires, which was so integral to Samhain. By the year 800, Irish Christians were celebrating all the saints and martyrs of the faith on November 1st, which became known as All Hallows' Day. All Hallows' Eve was, of course, October 31st, but there was a third day added called All Souls' Day on November 2nd. This three-day festival was known as Allhallowtide. This term is a bit unfamiliar to those who live outside of Europe, but it is still practiced in many Catholic communities today. Rather than making sure angry ghosts don't disrupt the harvest or harm people in the community, the saints and martyrs are remembered for their sacrifices and commemorated on these days.

The clever rebranding of celebrations that already existed was key in the rise of Christianity and the decline of paganism all over the world, but it is extremely obvious in Ireland.

Monks and Monasteries

Irish monks are often credited with recording and preserving historical records, and we know a lot more about medieval Ireland than we ever would without their dutiful studies and recording. These monks knew Latin and Greek, and they helped to disseminate spiritual teachings and guidance to each village. It was not uncommon for there to be small monastic communities on the borders of small kingships. The villagers would help the monks with farming, and the monks, in turn, would teach the villagers and help them with their problems. However, the drawback to this mostly peaceful and mutually beneficial arrangement was that if the kingships ever decided to go to battle, the monks were expected to join in. That was likely a surprise to these peaceful men the first time they had to hold a sword and shield.

Besides the many tiny monasteries, many of which do not survive today because of perishable building materials, there were great monasteries that do survive today. The largest of the Aran Islands off the coast of Galway, Inis Mór, is home to Ireland's oldest surviving monastery and likely the first one, St. Enda's Monastery. There is no longer a roof, but the structure of the building is clearly laid out, and it is a hugely popular site to visit because of its gorgeous location and the solemn history it represents.

Glendalough in Wicklow is home to the "Monastic City." This complex of religious buildings and monuments was founded by St. Kevin in the 6th century and receives between 500,000 and 750,000 visitors each year. Visitors can see the remains of the Round Tower, the monastery itself, and gorgeous decorated crosses, as well as some medieval churches in various conditions.

Chapter 15: Celtic and Pagan Influence in Modern Ireland

Through the Celts' long and storied history, we have witnessed their early start in Austria and Switzerland, watched them spread eastward and even south toward Turkey, and finally saw them settle in Éire, the land of the harp, epic myths, saints and scholars, where some of the most amazing stories, legends, and traditions the world has ever seen have come to life. The decline of the Celts and their traditional, nature-related practices did not mean the end of their culture entirely; it was simply an evolution.

Of course, chieftains made way for kings, who made way for the church, although they did enjoy autonomy for a while, especially against the English, who held Ireland in bondage for so long. One reason Celtic art, language, and stories are kept alive today is that they provided a binding agent for Irish nationalism, which became especially important in the 20th century as the battle for Irish independence from Britain became vehement and bloody.

One important reason for the survival of stories like those of Cú Chulainn, Tír na nÓg, and the legends of the Tuatha Dé Danann is because the Druids and chieftains told these stories to the monks, who then preserved them in manuscripts so that they survived for generations. The reasons for the differences between versions of the same legends have to do with who told them and where they were recorded, as each tribe likely had its own version.

Nowadays, in Irish schools, these stories, like the Children of Lir, the origin of the harp, and Celtic folklore, are taught. Why do schools bother with dusting off these ancient stories? What are they meant to convey? The easiest answer is that the Celts, through the different iterations of Celtic history (Bronze Age, Iron Age, and Middle Ages), managed to keep some cohesiveness of their culture, no matter what tribe they belonged to. For example, it took Germanic tribes much longer to unite than it did for the tribes of Ireland, who always considered themselves part of the same people. This is why, despite Roman rule coming to Britain and remaining there for centuries, Ireland was a much more difficult land to conquer politically. Religiously, though, the country submitted much more easily. This has a lot to do with the conviction of the missionaries and saints to the Emerald Isle, most notably Patrick.

The most obvious remnants of Celtic paganism are the celebration of festivals traditionally held between and on equinoxes and solstices, such as Samhain and Lughnasadh. These festivals are still held today, just with different names and no animal sacrifices. Candle lighting has been a prominent practice throughout history, both to honor the dead and to protect against the forces of darkness, and Catholics still do this, just like their pagan ancestors.

In the early 20th century, the harp became the national symbol of Ireland, a banner to unite separatists who were fighting the English for their freedom. The harp was on Irish money and is even still on euro coins. These freedom fighters (or terrorists, depending on your point of view) told stories about Finn MacCool, Cú Chulainn, the chieftainess Boudica, and all the gods and goddesses of the Celtic pantheon to bolster their courage and to stir nationalist fire within their hearts so that they could continue to fight for their land. Much like Native Americans, the Irish have always had a deep connection to the earth, and after centuries of building revered pagan holy sites and fighting for the land taken by conquerors, that connection does not easily leave. These sites, like Newgrange and other burial mounds, sacred mountaintops, and famous sites like the fabled stone where Cú Chulainn perished, became rallying points, physical, tangible things worth uniting over and fighting for.

Paganism and Christianity cross over in other ways. Often, Irish churches and Bibles are decorated with symbols like St. Brigid's cross (originally a pagan symbol for the goddess of the same name), Dara knots, shamrocks, and even the tree of life, a widely known and used symbol throughout many religious and cultural traditions. The trinity knot, or triquetra, is actually known to predate Christianity's arrival and has even been found in Norwegian churches dating from one thousand years ago. It is said to be one of the oldest surviving religious symbols. Although there are a few more popular persisting symbols, one of the most ancient is the triskele, the triple spiral, symbolizing things in groups of three. You have the choice of its meaning. The Christians use this ancient Celtic pagan symbol to represent the Father, Son, and Holy Spirit. The triskele can also be used to represent the earth, sea, and sky; past, present, and future; life, death, and rebirth; or any other triple element one can think of.

Triquetra.
https://commons.wikimedia.org/wiki/File:Triquetra-circle-interlaced.svg

In the 21st century, Celtic reconstructionist pagans, or Neopagans, are starting to revive their ancestral practices. Although the Republic of Ireland has long been known for its staunch conservative politics, even within the last few decades, it has really loosened up on a lot of its conservative politics and viewpoints (healthcare, abortion, marriage, immigration, etc.). There has also been a religious shift. Today, more than ever, modern Irish citizens either identify with atheism or have no religious affiliation at all. The Catholic population is still the majority, but those without religious affiliations are on the rise, as are those who wish to reclaim their heritage in the form of Celtic pagan practices.

Triskele.
https://commons.wikimedia.org/wiki/File:Triple-Spiral-Symbol.svg

Modern Irish pagans practice Samhain as similarly as they can to what their ancestors did, lighting two bonfires and walking between them to purify themselves. They also use the bonfires to toss in offerings of produce to the Dagda and the Morrigan. It is easier than it ever was to practice these traditions openly without fear of reprisal from oppressive authorities. Many Irish today practice the wedding traditions we mentioned in Chapter 11, holding ceremonies in sacred groves and having pagan shamans conduct these ceremonies, which are deeply connected with nature.

Conclusion

Simply walking around in Ireland, whether in a city, national park, or in nature, especially along the Cliffs of Moher, Newgrange, or the Giant's Causeway, one can feel its ancient traditions and beauty. It is easy to understand the connection the Druids and the ancient Celts felt to nature and the land, and it is understandable that the Irish fought tooth and nail to take back their beloved homeland.

The Celts of Ireland were proud warriors, but that does not mean they were ruthless and without compassion. Women had unprecedented rights during the Bronze Age and the Middle Ages. Despite their agricultural lifestyle, which did involve felling forests to make way for fields and pastures, the Celts held a deep respect for the environment around them and used sustainable farming practices and field demarcation that are used in Britain and Ireland to this day. They were healthy and robust people because of their varied and plentiful diet, which is one reason they thrived on Irish soil, despite the desolate and barren winter months on the island.

Legends and stories of creatures like the Dullahan, the Pooka, and the infamous banshee still abound in schools and homes. The Irish are still famed storytellers with a gift to weave great tales, and they have honed their skills with these legends all their lives. Every Irish child can recite tales about the Fair Folk and the Tuatha Dé Danann and its most famous members. Most Irish adults know the origin of the harp, the story of the Land of the Young, and the Tragedy of the Sons of Tuireann. These stories are not just stories—they give a voice and a picture of the national identity of those with fierce pride. This pride is justified, as it comes from a long line of warriors, sages, bishops, saints, scholars, freedom fighters, revolutionaries, poets, authors, historians, activists, musicians, and artists.

Although Irish Gaelic is definitely not the same language the Celts spoke, it is its grandchild. Through tracing the origins of words in Irish Gaelic, we can see the fingerprints of the Celts, and we can see through their eyes. Language often reveals the way that people see the world, and that is no less true when it comes to the Celts. This is also true for religious practices. By looking at Celtic art, we can see that they venerated plants and animals as essential to life, and they honored their gods by honoring nature with artwork they presented as offerings. The Celts believed their loved ones went on to an afterlife and that they would see them again, so they were sure to laden their graves with as many needed and beloved objects as they could. They also believed that Samhain was a special liminal time when the dead could visit them, and they cared for their dead by laying out food offerings for them in much the same way that people celebrate Día de los Muertos today.

Christianity has had a profound and lasting effect on Ireland and the people who called it home in the 5th century. There were some Christians there before, but they were likely slaves taken from other lands; they had no established community that early on. In spite of the clash of beliefs, the Celts managed to keep quite a few of their traditions when converting to Catholicism, which is another testament to Celtic and later Irish resilience and adaptability.

Why are the Celts so important? They ruled Ireland for about two millennia. Their belief system, marriage and death rituals, and festivals shaped the very land on which they chose to settle. The Celts are inseparable from Ireland, even though Gauls (who mixed with Franks and Normans, among others, to become the French) and Basque people are descendants of Celts. Scottish, Welsh, and Manx are all descendants of Celtic peoples as well, but it is the Irish Celts the world remembers the most clearly. This is partly because of the La Tène art that is so enduring and captivating. It is also because Celtic history and mythology were kept alive in writing, although we have lost quite a bit of it. And it is partly because the Celts managed to live on through what they left behind, archaeologically, artistically, poetically, and linguistically. They have left their indelible mark on the world, which is more than many ancient peoples can say. Who knows how many ancient cultures have vanished without a trace? But the Celts, whether they realized it or not, made their mark on the world.

By learning about the Celts and Irish history, we can learn about how Ireland became what it is today, and we can learn about how ancient people in western Europe conducted their lives. By learning about their traditions, we can see where many of our modern traditions originated. After all, more Irish people live in a diaspora overseas than in Ireland itself, and these are the Celts' descendants. They have kept the Celtic tradition alive in poetry, song, and family traditions they may not even be consciously aware of.

We hope you enjoyed this introduction to Celtic history, and we also hope that it has inspired you to delve deeper into whichever aspects spoke to you. There is so much more to know and discover about these mysterious and fascinating people.

Here's another book by Enthralling History that you might like

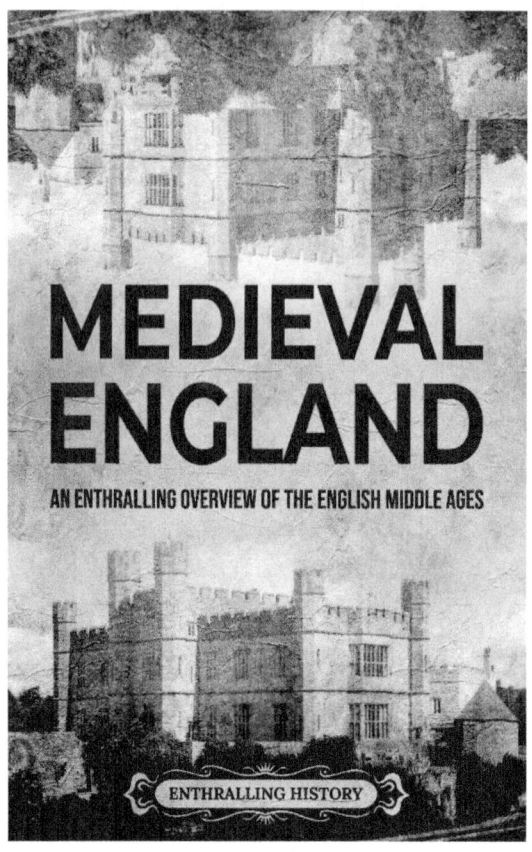

Free limited time bonus

Stop for a moment. We have a free bonus set up for you. The problem is this: we forget 90% of everything that we read after 7 days. Crazy fact, right? Here's the solution: we've created a printable, 1-page pdf summary for this book that you're reading now. All you have to do to get your free pdf summary is to go to the following website:

https://livetolearn.lpages.co/enthrallinghistory/

Once you do, it will be intuitive. Enjoy, and thank you!

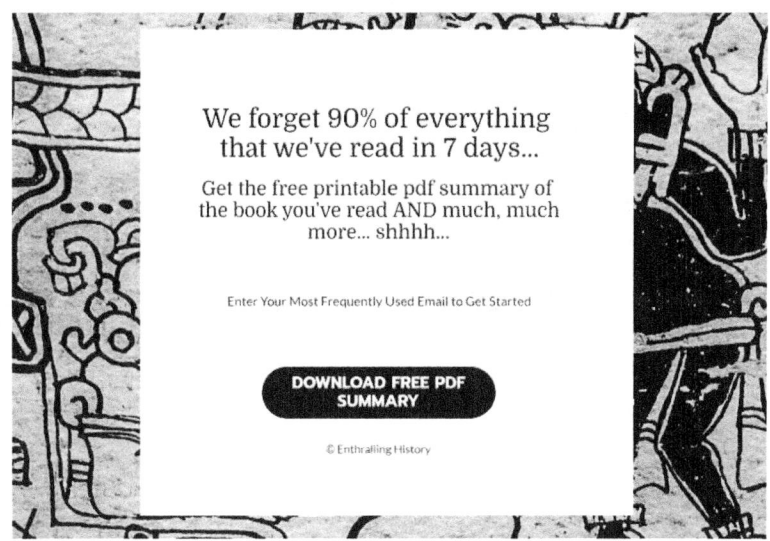

Works Cited

(IrishMyths.com), Posted byI. E. "Were There Female Druids?" *Irish Myths*, 14 Jan. 2023, https://irishmyths.com/2022/04/29/female-druids/

17, March, et al. "Who Was St. Patrick?" *Diocese of St. Augustine*, 17 Mar. 2022, https://www.dosafl.com/2022/03/17/who-was-st-patrick/?gclid=Cj0KCQjw8qmhBhClARIsANAtbocCRKLcgJRz8Y3uxPcO0sbIpQw9mInJbddIQf8WB75s2tV7PriTT1gaAuMZEALw_wcB

"8 Facts about the Celts." *History.com*, A&E Television Networks, https://www.history.com/news/celts-facts-ancient-europe

"Abhartach." *Wikipedia*, Wikimedia Foundation, 6 Feb. 2023, https://en.wikipedia.org/wiki/Abhartach

"Ancient Celtic Women." *Wikipedia*, Wikimedia Foundation, 14 Mar. 2023, https://en.wikipedia.org/wiki/Ancient_Celtic_women

"Ancient Celts Embalmed Enemy Heads as Trophies." *Nature News*, Nature Publishing Group, 9 Nov. 2018, https://www.nature.com/articles/d41586-018-07375-0

"AOS SÍ." *Wikipedia*, Wikimedia Foundation, 14 Mar. 2023, https://en.wikipedia.org/wiki/Aos_S%C3%AD#:~:text=Aos%20s%C3%AD%20(pronounced%20%5Bi%CB%90s%CB%A0%20%CB%88%CA%83i%CB%90,comparable%20to%20fairies%20or%20elves

"Balor." *Encyclopedia Britannica*, Encyclopedia Britannica, Inc., https://www.britannica.com/topic/Balor

"Beliefs, Practices, and Institutions." *Encyclopedia Britannica*, Encyclopedia Britannica, Inc., https://www.britannica.com/topic/Celtic-religion/Beliefs-practices-and-institutions

Bhagat, September 20. "The Origins and Practices of Mabon." *Boston Public Library*, https://www.bpl.org/blogs/post/the-origins-and-practices-of-mabon/

Bisdent. "Epona." *World History Encyclopedia*, Https://Www.worldhistory.org#Organization, 2 Apr. 2023, https://www.worldhistory.org/article/153/epona/

"Brigid." *Wikipedia*, Wikimedia Foundation, 7 Feb. 2023, https://en.wikipedia.org/wiki/Brigid.

"Cailleach - Irish Goddess of the Winter & Her Trail in Ireland." *IrishCentral.com*, 4 Jan. 2023, https://www.irishcentral.com/travel/best-of-ireland/cailleach-irish-goddess-winter-trail-ireland#:~:text=The%20Cailleach%20is%20the%20goddess,we%20celebrate%20today%20as%20Halloween

"Cailleach." *Wikipedia*, Wikimedia Foundation, 5 Mar. 2023, https://en.wikipedia.org/wiki/Cailleach

"Canola (Mythology)." *Wikipedia*, Wikimedia Foundation, 14 Apr. 2022, https://en.wikipedia.org/wiki/Canola_(mythology)#:~:text=In%20Irish%20mythology%2C%20Cana%20Cludhmor,stroll%20to%20clear%20her%20head

Cartwright, Mark. "Ancient Celts." *World History Encyclopedia*, https://www.worldhistory.org/#Organization, 5 Apr. 2023, https://www.worldhistory.org/celt/

Cartwright, Mark. "Cernunnos." *World History Encyclopedia*, https://www.worldhistory.org/#Organization, 4 Apr. 2023, https://www.worldhistory.org/Cernunnos/#:~:text=Cernunnos%20was%20an%20ancient%20Celtic,a%20torc%20around%20his%20neck

Cartwright, Mark. "The Morrigan." *World History Encyclopedia*, https://www.worldhistory.org/#Organization, 3 Apr. 2023, https://www.worldhistory.org/The_Morrigan/#:~:text=Appropriately%2C%20then%2C%20all%20three%20goddesses,of%20which%20contains%20a%20serpent

"Celt Timeline." *World History Encyclopedia RSS*, https://www.worldhistory.org/#Organization, https://www.worldhistory.org/timeline/celt/

"Celtic Calendar." *Wikipedia*, Wikimedia Foundation, 30 Mar. 2023, https://en.wikipedia.org/wiki/Celtic_calendar#:~:text=Among%20the%20Insular%20Celts%2C%20the,November%20in%20the%20modern%20calendar

"The Celtic Languages." *YouTube*, YouTube, 25 Dec. 2016, https://www.youtube.com/watch?v=ri1Vw3w1_10

"Celtic Metalwork Art (C.400 BCE - 100 CE)." *Celtic Metalwork Art: History, Characteristics of La Tene, Hallstatt Cultures,* http://www.visual-arts-cork.com/irish-crafts/celtic-metalwork-art.htm

"Celtic Religion - What Information Do We Really Have." *Celtic Religion - What Information Do We Really Have,* http://campus.murraystate.edu/academic/faculty/tsaintpaul/celtreli.html#BELIEFS%20IN%20CONNECTION%20TO%20CHILDREN

"Celtic Weapons: Art." *Celtic Weapons Art,* http://www.visual-arts-cork.com/cultural-history-of-ireland/celtic-weapons-art.htm

"Celts." *Wikipedia,* Wikimedia Foundation, 2 Apr. 2023, https://en.wikipedia.org/wiki/Celts

"CÚ Chulainn." *Wikipedia,* Wikimedia Foundation, 3 Apr. 2023, https://en.wikipedia.org/wiki/C%C3%BA_Chulainn#:~:text=C%C3%BA%20Chulainn%20(%2Fku%CB%90%CB%88,who%20is%20also%20his%20father

"CÚ Chulainn: The Legend of the Irish Hulk (Irish Mythology Explained)." *YouTube,* YouTube, 27 Apr. 2018, https://www.youtube.com/watch?v=GgHBGFL9v7s&feature=youtu.be

"The Dagda." *Wikipedia,* Wikimedia Foundation, 5 Mar. 2023, https://en.wikipedia.org/wiki/The_Dagda

Daly, Zoë "Who Is Ériu, the Patron Goddess of Ireland?" *Ériu,* Ériu, 21 Sept. 2022, https://eriu.eu/blogs/learn/eriu-patron-goddess-of-ireland

Dhruti Bhagat. April 30. "The Origins and Practices of Holidays: Beltane and the Last Day of Ridván." *Boston Public Library,* https://www.bpl.org/blogs/post/the-origins-and-practices-of-holidays-beltane-and-the-last-day-of-ridvan/#:~:text=Beltane%20is%20a%20Celtic%20word,well%20as%20increase%20their%20fertility

Dhruti Bhagat. June 18. "The Origins and Practices of Litha." *Boston Public Library,* https://www.bpl.org/blogs/post/the-origins-and-practices-of-litha/#:~:text=The%20Celts%20celebrated%20Litha%20with,the%20bonfires%20for%20good%20luck.&text=Other%20European%20traditions%20included%20setting,into%20a%20body%20of%20water

Did Iron Age Celts Really Hunt Wild Boar (Sus Scrofa)? - Jstor.org. https://www.jstor.org/stable/pdf/20557283.pdf

Dorn, Lori. "The Mythology behind the Royal Fairies of Celtic Lore." *Laughing Squid,* 13 June 2022, https://laughingsquid.com/supernatural-fairies-of-celtic-lore/#:~:text=The%20fairies%20of%20Celtic%20traditions,real%20ancient%20inhabitants%20of%20Ireland

"Druid." *Encyclopedia Britannica*, Encyclopedia Britannica, Inc., 15 Feb. 2023, https://www.britannica.com/topic/Druid

"Dullahan: The Headless Horseman of Irish Folklore - (Irish/Celtic Mythology Explained)." *YouTube*, YouTube, 14 Jan. 2019, https://www.youtube.com/watch?v=NEUCF-AA5WM

"Epona." *Encyclopedia Britannica*, Encyclopedia Britannica, Inc., https://www.britannica.com/topic/Epona

"Exploring Celtic Mythology: Children of Lir." *YouTube*, YouTube, 18 June 2018, https://www.youtube.com/watch?v=hROVjj0fX84

"Farming in Celtic Britain." *Roman Britain*, 26 Jan. 2023, https://www.roman-britain.co.uk/the-celts-and-celtic-life/farming-in-celtic-britain/

Fergus. "Tobernalt Holy Well, Sligo History." *The Irish Place*, 16 Feb. 2020, https://www.theirishplace.com/heritage/holy-wells/tobernalt-holy-well-sligo-history/

"Fomorians." *Wikipedia*, Wikimedia Foundation, 27 Dec. 2022, https://en.wikipedia.org/wiki/Fomorians

Gill, N.S. "Boudicca: A Mother's Revenge or Celtic Society's Laws?" *ThoughtCo*, ThoughtCo, 12 Aug. 2018, https://www.thoughtco.com/celtic-marriage-laws-4092652

"Glas Gaibhnenn." *Wikipedia*, Wikimedia Foundation, 4 Jan. 2023, https://en.wikipedia.org/wiki/Glas_Gaibhnenn#:~:text=Glas%20Gaibhnenn%20(Irish%3A%20Glas%20Gaibhnenn,yields%20profuse%20quantities%20of%20milk

"Goibniu." *Wikipedia*, Wikimedia Foundation, 10 Oct. 2022, https://en.wikipedia.org/wiki/Goibniu

hawk99. "History of Bees and Beekeeping - Bedtime History." *Bedtime History - Educational Stories, Podcasts, and Videos for Kids & Families*, 5 Oct. 2022, https://bedtimehistorystories.com/history-of-bees-and-beekeeping/

"Imbolc." *Wikipedia*, Wikimedia Foundation, 6 Mar. 2023, https://en.wikipedia.org/wiki/Imbolc

"Ireland in the Bronze Age." *Study.com | Take Online Courses. Earn College Credit. Research Schools, Degrees & Careers*, https://study.com/academy/lesson/ireland-in-the-bronze-age-life-houses-facts.html#:~:text=The%20average%20person%20in%20Bronze,break%20than%20any%20stone%20axes

"Irish Legends: Aine the Goddess Who Took Revenge on a King." *IrelandInformation.com*, https://www.ireland-information.com/irish-mythology/aine-irish-legend.html

Irish Monasticism,

http://www.earlychristianireland.net/Specials/Irish%20Monasticism/

"Irish People." *Wikipedia*, Wikimedia Foundation, 3 Apr. 2023, https://en.wikipedia.org/wiki/Irish_people

"Iron Age People: Celts." *Ask about Ireland*, https://www.askaboutireland.ie/learning-zone/primary-students/subjects/history/history-the-full-story/irelands-early-inhabitant/iron-age-people-celts/

Jaideep.krishnan. "The Arrival of Christianity in Ireland: The Romans and Saint Patrick." *Wondrium Daily*, 7 Aug. 2020, https://www.wondriumdaily.com/the-arrival-of-christianity-in-ireland-the-romans-and-saint-patrick/#:~:text=Roman%20Britain%20and%20the%20Spread%20of%20Christianity&text=Since%20Britain%20was%20very%20tightly,spread%20out%20into%20the%20countryside

Liao, Jenny. "Introduction to the Gaelic Languages: Glossika Blog." *The Glossika Blog*, The Glossika Blog, 3 May 2018, https://ai.glossika.com/blog/introduction-to-the-gaelic-languages

"Linguistics." *Exploring Celtic Civilizations*, https://exploringcelticciv.web.unc.edu/linguistics/

"Lugh." *Wikipedia*, Wikimedia Foundation, 10 Mar. 2023, https://en.wikipedia.org/wiki/Lugh

"Lughnasadh." *Wikipedia*, Wikimedia Foundation, 30 Mar. 2023, https://en.wikipedia.org/wiki/Lughnasadh

"Milesians." *Encyclopedia Britannica*, Encyclopedia Britannica, Inc., https://www.britannica.com/topic/Milesians

"Monastic City." *Glendalough, Co. Wicklow, Ireland*, 20 Apr. 2020, https://glendalough.ie/heritage/monastic-city/

Moody, Sabrina. "Meanwhile, in Ireland: Ostara." *The Comenian*, https://comenian.org/7527/news/meanwhile-in-ireland-ostara/

"Morrigan: The Fearless Celtic Goddess of War." *ConnollyCove*, 7 Mar. 2023, https://www.connollycove.com/morrigan-goddess-of-war/#:~:text=Ancient%20mythology%20tells%20us%20that,dressed%20in%20a%20red%20cloak

"Muiredach's Cross." *Muiredach's Cross, the West Cross and the North Cross at Monasterboice*, http://www.megalithicireland.com/High%20Cross%20Monasterboice.htm

"Ogham." *Wikipedia*, Wikimedia Foundation, 23 Mar. 2023, https://en.wikipedia.org/wiki/Ogham

O'Hara, Author Keith. "Dearg Due (Female Vampire): Irishman's 2023 Tale." *The Irish Road Trip*, 4 Jan. 2023, https://www.theirishroadtrip.com/dearg-due/

O'Hara, Author Keith. "The Banshee: Origin + What It Sounds like (2023)." *The Irish Road Trip*, 4 Jan. 2023, https://www.theirishroadtrip.com/the-banshee/

"Oidheadh Chlainne Tuireann." *Oxford Reference*, https://www.oxfordreference.com/display/10.1093/oi/authority.20110803100247501;jsessionid=E2B24DF9A20D347AA296ED414F8291EA

O'Neill, Brian. "Celts Arrive in Ireland - Iron Age Period - History of Ireland." *Your Irish Culture*, 1 Apr. 2023, https://www.yourirish.com/history/ancient/the-celts#:~:text=When%20the%20Celtic%20culture%20did,kingship%2C%20kingdoms%2C%20and%20power

"Pagan or Christian? Burial in Ireland during the 5th to 8th Centuries." *Home*, https://www.taylorfrancis.com/chapters/edit/10.4324/9781315087269-9/pagan-christian-burial-ireland-5th-8th-centuries-ad-brien-elizabeth

"Palladius (Medieval Ireland)." *Whatwhenhow RSS*, http://what-when-how.com/medieval-ireland/palladius-medieval-ireland/

"Pelagius." *Encyclopedia Britannica*, Encyclopedia Britannica, Inc., https://www.britannica.com/biography/Pelagius-Christian-theologian

"Pliny the Elder." *Encyclopedia Britannica*, Encyclopedia Britannica, Inc., https://www.britannica.com/biography/Pliny-the-Elder

Published by Tori On 9th August 2019. "All about Celtic Weddings- History, Handfasting and More! ★ Unconventional Wedding." *Unconventional Wedding*, 3 Apr. 2023, https://unconventionalwedding.co.uk/celtic-weddings-history-handfasting-and-more/

"PÚCA." *Wikipedia*, Wikimedia Foundation, 25 Mar. 2023, https://en.wikipedia.org/wiki/P%C3%BAca#:~:text=The%20p%C3%BAca%20(Irish%20for%20spirit,hinder%20rural%20and%20marine%20communities

Quinn, Eimear. "Irish Language Guide." *Wilderness Ireland*, 31 Mar. 2022, https://www.wildernessireland.com/blog/irish-language-guide/

"Sacred Grove." *Wikipedia*, Wikimedia Foundation, 25 Mar. 2023, https://en.wikipedia.org/wiki/Sacred_grove#:~:text=The%20Celts%20used%20sacred%20groves,Druids%20oversaw%20such%20rituals

"Saint Patrick." *Wikipedia*, Wikimedia Foundation, 28 Mar. 2023, https://en.wikipedia.org/wiki/Saint_Patrick

"Samhain." *Wikipedia*, Wikimedia Foundation, 16 Mar. 2023, https://en.wikipedia.org/wiki/Samhain

"Shield: British Museum." *The British Museum*, https://www.britishmuseum.org/collection/object/H_1857-0715-1

"Sluagh." *Emerald Isle Irish and Celtic Myths, Fairy Tales and Legends,* https://emeraldisle.ie/sluagh

"St Patrick's Purgatory." *Wikipedia*, Wikimedia Foundation, 12 Mar. 2023, https://en.wikipedia.org/wiki/St_Patrick%27s_Purgatory#:~:text=had%20substantial%20proof.-,St.,believe%20all%20that%20he%20said

"The Story of Tír Na Nóg." *YouTube*, YouTube, 12 Feb. 2018, https://www.youtube.com/watch?v=cSp-ihnpJ64

"Strabo." *Encyclopedia Britannica,* Encyclopedia Britannica, Inc., https://www.britannica.com/biography/Strabo

Thompson, Chris. "Pleasing the 'King-of-Bling!" ~ Notes on the Tasks of the Sons of Tuireann." *Pleasing the "King-of-Bling!" ~ Notes on the Tasks of the Sons of Tuireann – Story Archaeology,* 4 May 2014, https://storyarchaeology.com/pleasing-the-king-of-bling-notes-on-the-tasks-of-the-sons-of-tuireann/

"Traditional Irish Fishing Methods." *National Museum of Ireland,* https://www.museum.ie/en-IE/Collections-Research/Folklife-Collections/Folklife-Collections-List-(1)/Fishing-and-Hunting/Traditional-Irish-fishing-methods#:~:text=Traps%20made%20of%20wicker%20or,salmon%20took%20place%20under%20licence

"Tír Na Nóg." *Wikipedia,* Wikimedia Foundation, 4 Feb. 2023, https://en.wikipedia.org/wiki/T%C3%ADr_na_n%C3%93g

"Wheel of the Year." *Wikipedia*, Wikimedia Foundation, 1 Apr. 2023, https://en.wikipedia.org/wiki/Wheel_of_the_Year

"Who Were the Celts?" *Museum Wales,* https://museum.wales/articles/1341/Who-were-the-Celts/#:~:text=Where%20did%20the%20Celts%20come,and%20into%20the%20Czech%20Republic

World, Author Irish Around The. "Top 20 Irish Celtic Symbols and Their Meanings Explained." *Irish Around the World,* 19 Jan. 2022, https://irisharoundtheworld.com/celtic-symbols/

Printed in Great Britain
by Amazon